PRINCIPLES OF VISUAL PERCEPTION

PRINCIPLES OF VISUAL PERCEPTION

CAROLYN M. BLOOMER

 VAN NOSTRAND REINHOLD COMPANY
New York Cincinnati Toronto London Melbourne

To Douglas G. Christie
and to the students at Parish Hill
this book is lovingly dedicated.

For contributing in special ways to the writing of this book I wish to thank Charles W. Avery, Carole Ann Bauer, Beth Beede, Richard Bloomer, Doris Davis, Janet Erickson, the Hartford Art School, I-Hsiung Ju, Lynn E. Stauffer, Jr., Wendy Lochner, and Nancy Newman Green.

Published in 1976 by Van Nostrand Reinhold Company
A Division of Litton Educational Publishing, Inc.
450 West 33rd Street
New York, N.Y. 10001

Van Nostrand Reinhold Limited
1410 Birchmount Road
Scarborough, Ontario M1P 2E7, Canada

Van Nostrand Reinhold Australia Pty. Ltd.
17 Queen Street
Mitcham, Victoria 3132, Australia

Van Nostrand Reinhold Company Ltd.
Molly Millars Lane
Wokingham, Berkshire, England

16 15 14 13 12 11 10 9 8 7 6 5 4 3 2 1

Library of Congress Cataloging in Publication Data

Bloomer, Carolyn.
   Visual perception.

   Bibliography: p.
   Includes index.
   SUMMARY: Surveys the principles of visual perception based on psychological research and everyday experience, and how they are related to the perception of art in particular.
      1. Visual perception.   2. Composition (Art)
3. Optical illusions.   [1. Visual perception.
2. Optical illusions.   3. Art appreciation]   I. Title.
BF241.B57 1976   152.1'4   74-27757
ISBN 0-442-20825-1

CONTENTS

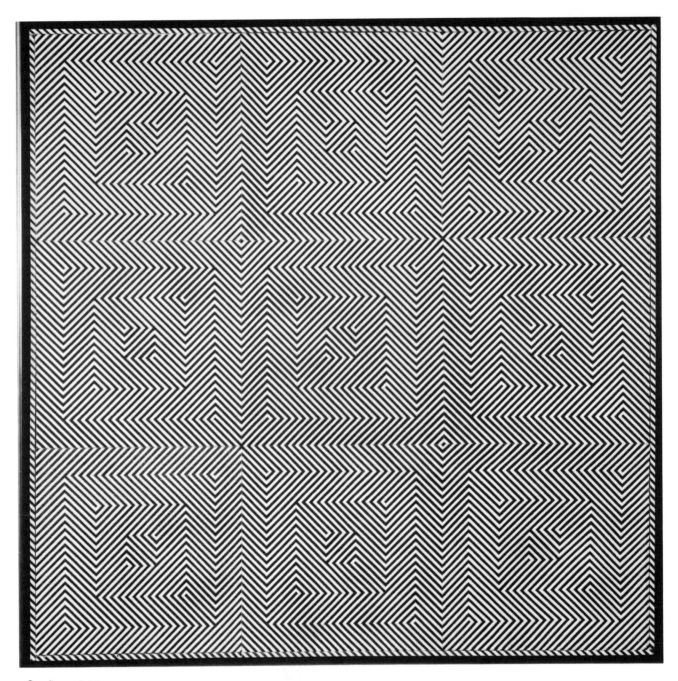

See figure 3-17.

INTRODUCTION

My purpose in writing this book was to put together a comprehensive summary of the principles of visual perception, based on psychological research as well as on familiar everyday experience, and to relate these principles to art in particular. I have not dealt with the more erudite issues in perception, which are multitudinous, but the perceptive reader will recognize many profound implications.

This book was born—as are many books—of dissatisfaction and need. The longer I taught art and the more I talked with people about art, the more I encountered a fundamental lack in understanding *what happens when a human being looks at something*. It is to this question that this book is addressed.

In my experience as a teacher I have found that when students become knowledgeable about the processes of visual perception, they can begin to make sound, independent evaluations of their own work as well as the work of others. Such understanding is as essential for looking at art as for making it. When students work on specific perceptual problems, their projects take on focus and energy, and they constantly discover personally relevant connections with historical and contemporary art—they find dimensions of meaning.

The problem of meaning has profound significance for the individual—whether student, artist, or viewer. Perception is ruthlessly parsimonious: we tune out, forget, or berate anything that lacks meaning for us. The benign neglect of visual education by our schools has served to perpetuate the myth that the process of seeing is essentially objective and unlearned, and so for many people today art appears irrelevant. As a practicing artist I am deeply concerned about the effect of this on the public's relationship to its artists. For this reason the book also addresses itself to the general reader in the hope of enlarging the "comfort zone" between artist and viewer.

1-1. How many different things can you see in this inkblot?
(Permission Joyce Burnham and Rachel Robertson.)

1. MEANING:

The First Step in Understanding Your Mind

The human mind *uncontrollably* creates meaning from stimuli. This is a fact, a process you cannot escape, an activity that goes on in spite of your will or even your desire. Your mind constantly projects meaning onto things—sometimes meanings that are not there, meanings that are complete figments of your imagination.

You can easily watch your mind in action with the following experiment. If you can get a small group of people together to share the experience, it will prove even more exciting. Eliminating all words, cut out about fifteen or twenty pictures from magazines, particularly of interesting people or scenes. Then cut out an equal number of words or phrases; advertisements are a good source. Keeping the groups separate, turn the picture and word pieces face down, and scramble each group. Pair each picture piece with a phrase piece while they are still face down. Then turn over the pairs. The results may shock and astound you, for more than half the pairs will seem to have some meaning, often humorous or ironic. The results are so uncanny that it may appear as if someone had planned it—and yet the combinations are completely random, left to the laws of chance. The results seem far above the expectations of chance. Why?

The human mind is extremely creative about this business of making meaning, sometimes to the extent that no meaning may be intended or found—*except in the mind of the beholder.* Exercising this creative function of the mind is part of such popular activities as astrology, tarot cards, the I-Ching, handwriting analysis, UFO speculations, and even such respectable procedures as the Rorschach test, the infamous inkblots used by psychologists to analyze personality.

This miracle of the mind's drive toward meaning exists from the first day of life. Scientific studies show that infants as young as one to fourteen days of age prefer to look at patterned cards rather than plain ones. Infants between one and fifteen weeks of age find complex patterns (stripes, bull's-eyes, or checkerboards) more interesting than simpler ones (crosses, circles, or triangles). Infants also enjoy looking at spheres more than at flat circles. After four months of age babies respond consistently and significantly more often to patterns resembling the configuration of a human face than to patterns of scrambled features, and they look least often at a featureless control pattern.

Obviously, a baby's survival is involved more with the human face than with any other stimulus: a face has more *meaning* for him. Interestingly enough, people never lose their eagerness to perceive the configuration of a human face—even in the most unlikely situations (Figure 1-3). Is this scanning for meaning the extension of a survival strategy that has its beginnings in infancy?

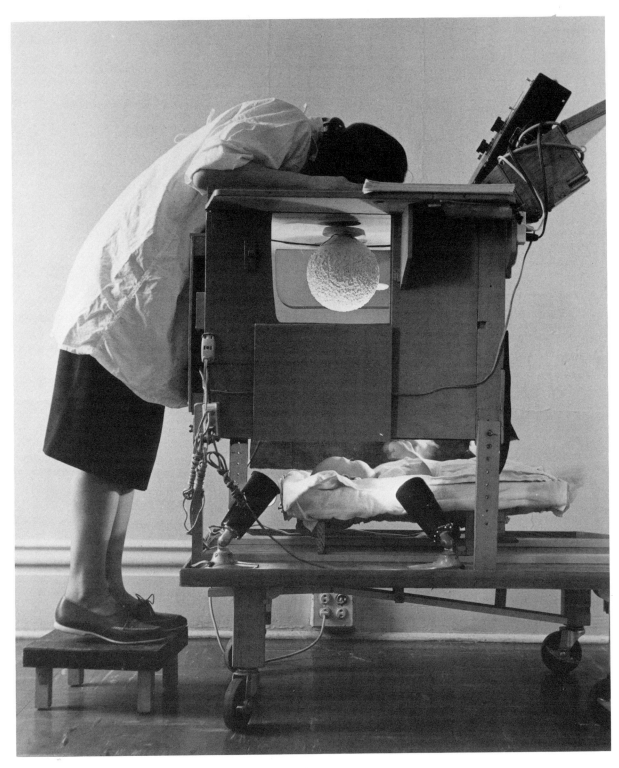

1-2. Chamber for observing infant responses to visual stimuli.
(Photograph by David Linton permission *Scientific American*.)

The need for meaning even affects the efficiency of our mental processes. Many studies show that people memorize words much faster than nonsense syllables and also that they forget nonsense syllables more quickly. People recognize patterns like 4357 more easily than patterns like ⌊₁ ₂⌐/, even though both are composed of identical elements. Memory-improvement techniques often involve creating meaningful images to associate with meaningless patterns such as telephone or social-security numbers. For example, the number four might stand for a table with four legs, the number five for a hand, and the number seven for a policeman with his arm out. The number 547 could then be coded by the image of a gigantic hand holding a table with a traffic policeman standing on top of it. To remember the number, you would first have to recall the "meaningful" image and then decode it. Such devices seem to involve more conscious effort than that required to directly recall a simple number; in relation to energy output they appear inefficient. However, the fact that such memory aids have proved effective for millions of people reveals the overwhelming importance of meaning for the human mind.

If your mind is so constantly preoccupied with the search for meaning, how will it respond if it does not find meaning? To answer this question, consider how you react when someone asks you a riddle or a mind-teasing problem and then walks away, refusing to tell you the answer. Do you have trouble getting it out of your mind? Do you find yourself going back to it again and again and again—almost against your will? Do you end up cursing (publicly or privately) the person who boggled your mind with this stupid problem? What about those awful wooden puzzles that, once apart, cannot seem to be put back together? How do you feel when confronted with a puzzle that you absolutely cannot solve? I feel frustrated, anxious, even angry.

1-3. A decaying taillight. (Photograph by Fred H. Stocking.)

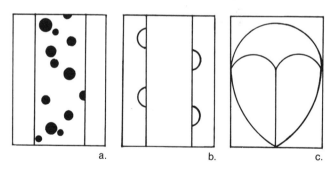

1-4. Droodles.

Droodle puzzles were popular at one time: they spread across the country like moron and elephant jokes. Figure 1-4 shows some sample droodles; try to figure out what they are. The answers are given at the end of the chapter. How long can you wait before looking them up? This may tell you something about your own ability to tolerate lack of meaning. When you do find out the answers, you may laugh—many people do. Why is laughter a common reaction? Because lack of meaning makes you tense, perhaps annoyed. But when the answer provides your mind with the meaning it needs, you are relieved, and your laughter discharges the energy that formed the tension. Laughter always expresses tension release.

People actually seem to *enjoy* this pattern of frustration followed by tension release. Multimillion-dollar businesses depend on the perennial willingness of people to put themselves in situations of looking for meaning and then finding it: jigsaw puzzles, crossword puzzles, cryptograms, anagrams, quiz shows, mystery stories, suspense movies, and so on. Of course, in all these situations you are secure in thinking that a meaningful answer exists. The crossword puzzle *does* have a solution, the wooden puzzle *can* go back together, the shaggy-dog story *will* have a punch line, and the mystery writer or movie director eventually *will* make everything fall into place (except for tricky stories such as *The Lady or the Tiger* and certain new-wave movies such as *Blow Up*).

But life is not always such a neat package. Sometimes you miss the crossword-puzzle solution. Sometimes people ask you unanswerable questions: Which came first, the chicken or the egg? If a tree falls in the forest and no one is around to hear it, is there any sound? How can your mind handle problems with no solution? One alternative is to ignore the problem, to tune out. Your mind overlooks that particular thing—pretends it doesn't exist. A good example of tuneout is demonstrated by the *new-word phenomenon*. When you learn a new word, it seems that you suddenly encounter the word everywhere: you talk to people who use it; you hear it on television, run across it in reading, find it in a crossword puzzle. Can the whole world suddenly be using this word just because *you* happened to learn it? No—the word was always used, but you ignored it: you overlooked it because it had no meaning for you. When suddenly it does have meaning, you no longer tune it out, you no longer overlook it. You perceive it.

Most people have many experiences like this.

Something is called to your attention, you learn something new, and you go around in a state of amazement that you had never noticed it before. A girl going with a boy who is involved with cars suddenly finds that automobiles, which before seemed more or less alike, now have important differences in manufacturers, designs, or engine refinements. Likewise, fishermen may talk for hours about variations among lures and baits, while people who are not interested in fishing quickly become bored and tune out. The same is true for many subjects: sports, business, switchblades, babies, rock music, politics, organic foods, operations, modern art. If you are not interested in it—if it has no meaning for you—you will tune it out.

Sometimes you are not allowed to tune out: the situation is too important to ignore. You usually go through life with a certain amount of security about things: the floor is not going to jump up at you; the ceiling is not going to fall in; the car will go in the direction in which you steer it; water will come out of the faucet when you turn it on. If these things don't happen, you look for the reason why: the meaning. Usually you can find it: there was an earthquake; a tie-rod broke; the well went dry.

The worst situations are those in which you cannot tune out nor find a meaningful answer. A classic example is a television repairman who thinks he has fixed the set—only it doesn't work. A common reaction would be to turn the situation over and over in his mind, repeating the steps he has already taken, hoping to find something he overlooked. When he has exhausted these possibilities, he will probably become very frustrated and may even express his anger by verbally or physically abusing the set. Even though this may make him feel better, it doesn't usually remedy the situation. The problem is still there: the set still doesn't work. Situations such as this, where you know something is wrong yet can't find an explanation, have been called by one psychologist *crazy-making*.[1] A famous turn-of-the-century play was based on a situation in which a husband drove his wife insane by gradually lowering the gaslights and then denying to her that they were any dimmer. The name of the play was *Gaslight*, and as a result of its popularity this particular brand of crazy-making came to be called *gaslighting.*

Some people deal with life the way the frustrated repairman deals with the television set. Repeating over and over steps that have worked in the past is termed *compulsive behavior* by psychiatrists and psychologists. Expressing anger through verbal or physical abuse is given such names as *overt hostility* or *hostile aggression.* Not being able to solve problems generates *frustration* and *anxiety.* People who are frustrated by an inability to make meaning out of really important experiences in their lives may end up doing things like committing suicide or homicide; attributing the bad or good things that happen to them to a plot, conspiracy, or divine plan (*paranoia, delusions of grandeur*); or withdrawing into a life of pure fantasy where they can completely control meaning (*schizophrenia*).

Most people can tolerate a certain amount of meaninglessness in their lives—indeed, you must develop this ability in order to survive. Certain people, however, seem to have an unusual ability to withstand—or even to prefer—a larger amount of disorder and chaos than normal: highly creative and productive artists, writers, and scientists. Studies of such people suggest that they are able to generate unusual or "new" meanings from stimuli considered chaotic or disordered by most people.

The innovator in any field, because of his very nature, has found that certain conventional orders and rules are unable to satisfy his needs for meaning. Instead, he feels he must create his own structure of meaning. This accounts for certain stereotypes such as the "crazy artist" and the "mad scientist."

The average person does not usually share an innovator's need for new meanings and, indeed, feels significantly more comfortable with familiar meanings that do not boggle his mind. Consequently, new scientific theories often meet strong public opposition (for example, Galileo's sun-centered universe and Darwin's theory of evolution). Almost all innovations in art have met with similar hostility: How can you call that art! My five-year-old could do that! They could hang it upside down and nobody would know the difference! I like a painting that looks like something! Lack of faith in artists is nothing new. Even a respectable critic of the late 1800s reacted to a show of impressionist paintings by saying, "You might as well give a monkey a paintbox!" Because of the peculiar way in which artists are viewed in our society, people do not feel as secure with an artist's work as they do, for instance, with the work of a mystery writer. They are often not at all certain that contemporary art *has* a meaning, and their negative reactions are a way of tuning out the problem.

1-5. Robert Morse (age 11). *Overload.* (Permission of the artist.)

One way to find meaning in art is to approach it in the same way as you approach other puzzles: with the faith that an answer, a meaning, *is* there, but you have to find it. You can do this in several ways. Many exhibitions have catalogs, and you can read these—do it before viewing if possible. Go to the gallery with some friends and share thoughts and reactions; several heads are better than one. Don't be afraid to ask questions of the museum or gallery attendant; most people enjoy showing off their knowledge and giving you their opinions. Above all, remember that the artist is reacting in a personal way to the human condition that we all share: the need to create meaning in his life.

1-6. Gallery visitors talk with the owner. (Permission Hayloft Galleries, Norwich, Connecticut. Photograph by Bruce Thompson.)

We have explored the fact that the mind is driven to find meaning, that it needs meaning in order to survive, and that it can be very creative in finding meaning. As the mind goes about organizing meaning, it operates according to a fundamental principle. Psychologists in the field of perception have established that the mind will find the simplest possible meaning to fit the facts. This principle is called the *law of simplicity*. Let us observe the way it works: look at Figure 1-7 and identify it. Is it a circle? Not really: it is not complete. Is it an incomplete circle or a circular line? Look again. It is somewhat irregular: a little squarish here, a little lumpy there. Oh well, you sigh. It is just a clumsy drawing of a circle—of an incomplete circle, that is.

Isn't it interesting that you keep calling it a circle? Oh yes, you can qualify that: an incomplete circle or a clumsy circle or an incomplete, clumsy circle—but you do keep referring to it as a circle. Since it is lumpy and irregular and thus not really circular, why not invent a new name for it? What will you call Figure 1-8? A circle with a piece out of it?

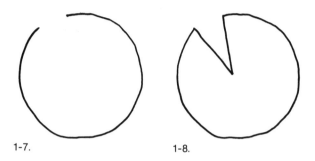

1-7.   1-8.

A circle with a part missing? It really is difficult, isn't it, to talk about these forms in terms other than circle terms? No matter what you say about them, you're always using words that refer to circular qualities. This is an example of the law of simplicity: a circle is the simplest category of meaning that your mind can come up with to fit the stimulus.

The law of simplicity is so basic that it has been codified in science as the *law of parsimony*, which states that the best scientific explanation is the simplest one that fits the data. How this law creates scientific progress is illustrated by a familiar example. At one time the earth was thought to be the center of the universe (Ptolemy's theory). But as more observations were collected, it became very difficult and complicated to continue explaining the solar system according to this theory. A theory proposed by Copernicus—that the sun was the center of the solar system—was a much simpler explanation of the facts. At the time this theory met strong opposition, because it caused serious theological problems related to the meaning of human existence. In fact, Galileo's development and defense of the Copernican theory led to his terrible persecution by the clergy. Ultimately, however, the theory that was consistent with the law of parsimony was the one that survived. The law of parsimony remains a basic criterion for scientific thought.

This principle was first applied to the workings of the human mind by a group of psychologists who pioneered a good deal of research into human perception, the Gestalt psychologists. *Gestalt* is a German word that means "form." Not only did the Gestaltists find that the mind perceives the simplest possible form, but also that it tends to see the "best" or most "correct" possible form. This means that you tend to see things not as they are—but as your mind thinks they ought to be.

This tendency explains why you were willing to make mental corrections of the irregular, incomplete circular stimulus and call it a circle. Probably you didn't even notice the irregularities until I called your attention to them; you may have dismissed them almost instantly with the fleeting, half-conscious explanation that the line was not intended to be irregular, that the artist was clumsy. Overlooking or tuning out the irregularities makes it easier to categorize the form as a circle.

This strong tendency of the mind to "correct" stimuli can sometimes cause problems. It might explain that old saying, "Love is blind." And it explains why proofreading is a difficult task: your mental "correcting" tends to tune out the very errors you are looking for. In one study the word "chack" was placed in two different contexts. In a sentence about poultry raising it was misread as "chick"; in a sentence about banking, it was misread as "check."

What is
wrong with this
this line?

According to the Gestaltists, we perceive whole configurations before becoming aware of details or component parts. In fact, in psychological terminology the word *gestalt* has come to be synonymous with "whole" or "total pattern." In everyday life your mind forms gestalts so rapidly that they seem to appear instantaneously, and you are not conscious of the process by which your mind forms them. As you read this, for example, you are perceiving words and phrases—not individual letters. Only when you are confronted with something new or unusual do you become aware of the processes going on inside your head as your mind struggles to grasp the meaning or gestalt (biw us tge tune fir akk giid neb ti cine ti tge aud if tgeur ciybtrt, for instance).

What are these processes by which the mind organizes meaning? First, you must become conscious that something is there. A stimulus must attract your attention before you can pay attention to it. For example, if you are driving at night, such an awareness might first appear as a sense of something seen out of the corner of your eye in your peripheral vision; it might be the shape or motion of something that is not where you expected it to be.

Second, your mind will differentiate the stimulus from its surroundings. You will decide what is the stimulus and what is not the stimulus (what is the rabbit and what is the road). In perception this is called establishing a *figure/ground relationship*.

Third, your mind will focus on the thing itself: its outline, size, color, texture, volume, etc. If you think of your mind as a computer, this represents the point at which you have punched the card and fed it into the computer, which then lights up and clicks away to arrive at an answer. Your brain sorts through past experience—categories of similar stimuli—and tries to come up with a meaning. Your mind's functioning—unlike that of a computer—is affected by fears and anxieties (*perceptual vigilance and defense*), as well as by positive rewards that you need and want (*wish fulfillment*).

Finally, if all goes well, your mind classifies and identifies the stimulus. You could call this the *Eureka!* or *I see!* step; the Gestaltists call it *closure*. Depending on the importance of the problem, closure is often accompanied by varying feelings of relief.

Closure frequently includes naming the stimulus. How much better people feel when they have a name for something is a peculiar phenomenon: naming often gives a powerful sense of relief and closure. Nothing is better proof of this than listening to little children between the ages of three and five when they ask lots of questions, mostly "What is that?" Even if you give a child only the name of the thing, he obviously experiences closure. What is that big light in the sky? That is called the moon. The Moon! The Moon! I see The Moon! When you stop to think about it, he doesn't really know anything more about the moon than before he asked the question. He just has a new combination of sounds with which to think or talk about it. Similarly, sick people often feel better when the doctor attaches a scientific name to their symptoms.

Schools are marvelous places to collect names for things. How much of your education consists simply of learning to name things correctly? People who memorize names and labels for things usually do well on tests and earn good grades, even though—like the child—they may not understand much more about reality than they did before.

Many respectable adult activities are based on the positive feelings that come from identifying or naming something: consider such hobbies as bird watching, stamp collecting, rock hunting, or antique collecting. The payoff comes when you are able to identify the stimulus. Some specialists in classification and naming have very practical functions: for example, medical pathologists, aerial-reconaissance pilots, geologists, anthropologists, police detectives, critics, commentators, and repairmen.

After you have classified and identified something, your mind usually turns off that stimulus and goes on to something else. This is another important principle of perception: the mind will see only as much as is necessary to obtain meaning or closure. Once closure has occurred, the stimulus becomes boring, the viewer uninterested. You express this when you find yourself saying such things as, "Oh, no, not that again!" or "How dull, another rerun!" or "You've seen one, you've seen 'em all!"

One of the achievements of a great artist is that his work provides a kind of renewable closure. This weighs in a very delicate balance: if the work is too simple, people will see, identify, turn off, and move on to something else very rapidly. On the other hand, if the work is too obscure, people cannot make closure and will also tune out and move away. One characteristic of really great art is that it provides enough stimulus for partial closure but not enough to completely turn you off. You sometimes hear people say, "I like that piece because every time I look at (listen to, read) it, I find something new." This quality is due not only to the meaning the artist *has* expressed but also to dimensions of meaning that he has withheld and that you, the viewer, project from your own experience. As long as the meaning derived from the artwork remains elastic enough to accommodate changes in your own experience, you will continue to find meaning reflected in it. For this reason you may find that at some times in your life you are more responsive to certain works than at other times. Possibilities for such renewable closure are inherent in the work of all great artists—Bach, Rembrandt, da Vinci, Michelangelo, Shakespeare, to name a few.

Advertising and commercial art most often fail to be great art because their purpose is quite different. They are designed first of all to attract your attention—to make you aware of the stimulus. If the advertiser cannot accomplish this, anything else he does is meaningless. Because of this our highways, marketplaces, and television screens become a jumble of bold, attention-getting devices. Secondly, such art needs to have your attention only long enough to get its message across: it needs to involve you only until you make closure. "Instant closure" is often accomplished with simple patterns such as circles, squares, triangles, letters of optimum legibility, and other visual patterns that quickly and clearly relate to past associations. Trademarks and traffic symbols are good examples of instant closure.

From a historical perspective it is interesting to note that the most popular art of the sixties provided less complex, faster, and more complete perceptual closure than earlier western art or oriental art. We should not be surprised to find that the consumption of art is consistent with other aspects of life: we eat prepackaged dinners, change residence every five years, fly across the continent in four hours, and push buttons to accomplish complex tasks. We are subjected to incessant visual training by advertising, marketing, and the mass media. Artists of the seventies, however, appear to reflect a disenchantment with this type of existence. Their "dematerialization" of art is focusing on personal and qualitative aspects of human experience, a focus that is becoming increasingly important in other sectors of our society as well.

Answers to droodles (Figure 1-4): a giraffe going by a second-story window; a bear going up the other side of a tree; and a fat lady on the end of a diving board.

1-9. Instant closure in the service of safety.

2-1. René Magritte. *Portrait.* Oil, 28⅞ by 19⅞ inches, 1935.
(Collection The Museum of Modern Art, New York. Gift of Kay
Sage Tanguy.)

2. VISION:

In the Eye of the Beholder

Most people are startled when they first see the painting reproduced in Figure 2-1. The presence of a human eye out of context immediately generates tension. An eye means much more to us than a simple instrument for gathering light rays. Images such as this affect us on a personal level.

Eye contact is a basic way of establishing communication with another person. If you doubt this, try to carry on a conversation with another person while constantly avoiding eye contact:

look behind him,

slightly to one side,

at the tip of his nose,

or at the tops of his ears.

This strategy is almost guaranteed to cause the other person a great deal of helpless frustration. At some time or other you have talked with someone who seemed to avoid your eyes. Can you recall your feelings about the experience? Isn't it as if something prevents genuine communication, as if you are not really in touch with each other? We place so much value on eye contact that we even use it as an index to a person's total character. In our culture we tend to believe that a person is telling the truth if he can look you straight in the eye and that a shifty-eyed person is hiding something and must have ulterior motives. You are so sensitive to eye contact that you quickly become aware of its absence. On television, for instance, you know immediately when someone is reading from cue cards. Experienced television personalities, by contrast, seem to look directly at you through the camera.

Researchers have found that eye contact is used for a good deal of unspoken communication. You can watch this the next time you walk down a street or along the corridor of a building where many people are coming and going. How do people avoid running into one another (most of the time, anyway)? They move according to rituals of eye contact, silent interchanges performed automatically and unconsciously. Look for them.

Cultures have strict and often differing rules about eye contact. In our culture strangers must not give each other more than a cursory, impersonal glance. If you are in a public place such as a bus, subway, or elevator and notice a stranger who keeps looking at you, you may feel uneasy, for a person who transgresses the usual rules of eye contact creates an uncomfortable, unpredictable situation. On the other hand eye contact in a romantic situation generates chemistry, electricity: "Our eyes met and instantly I knew...", or "he gazed deep into her eyes ....". Eye contact, then, is a signal, a prelude, an invitation to further interaction. Indeed, establishing eye contact is the first goal of therapists dealing with autistic children who have completely withdrawn from outside reality.

19

2-2. Romare Bearden. *The Conjur Woman.* Collage, 12⅛ by 9⅜ inches, 1964. (Collection The Museum of Modern Art, New York. Blanchette Rockefeller Fund.)

VISION: THE PRIME EXPERIENCE

References to vision weave through the fabric of our everyday language. Henry Ford was a man of *vision*. Love is *blind*. Oh, now I *see*! We *shut our eyes* to the truth, *keep an eye out*, *see eye-to-eye*, exchange *views*, become *all eyes*. We refer to things as *easy on the eyes*, *sights for sore eyes*, *eye-openers*, *eye-catchers*. People are *eyewitnesses*, *private eyes*, *seers*. We have *bull's-eyes*, *eyes of needles* and *storms*, *black-eyed peas*, and *eye of round*. Most of these examples do not refer to any physical aspect of vision—indeed, a literal interpretation is absurd: how do you keep an eye *out*, or become *all* eyes? Does an eye-catcher look like a flycatcher or a dogcatcher?

The process of visual perception is so basic and so profound an experience in human existence that we are compelled to articulate important mental activities or relationships in terms of vision. To *see* something is to understand it. To *have a viewpoint* is to take a conceptual position. To *look into something* is to investigate it.

People who have been blind from birth must experience profound alienation, not only because of their physical handicap but also because of the language with which we express many concepts. Imagine a blind child learning to read with, "Look, look. Oh, look. See Spot. See Spot run." Blind people are sometimes said to have a "sixth sense."

Eye contact alerts us to expect that other events may follow. Perhaps this is one reason why Magritte's painting (Figure 2-1) is so disconcerting. Meeting the eye (no pun intended!) triggers an automatic, unconscious preparation for something to happen. Simultaneously, however, we recognize that expectation as preposterous and discharge our tension with a laugh. A more serious use of eye contact in an artwork is shown in Figure 2-2. In this collage the eyes draw our attention and provide a focus or center for the work. Cover the eyes with your finger, and you will see what I mean. The classic recruiting poster from 1917 (Figure 2-3) also derives its impact from simulated eye contact, in this instance through the penetrating gaze of Uncle Sam. The power of certain individuals to cast spells by means of their gaze alone (the evil eye) is an almost universal superstition.

In Byzantium and Ethiopia evil persons in paintings were "never shown looking out of the picture for fear their evil eye might harm [the viewer]."[1]

In addition to communicating, eyes provide information about a person's psychological or physical condition. Fatigue, listlessness, excitement, fear, hostility, dreaminess—these and other states can all be signaled by the appearance of a person's eyes. You immediately identify a person with unmoving, staring eyes as seriously abnormal. A vacant stare is characteristic of idiocy, death, catatonia, shell shock, and other extreme traumas.

2-3. James Montgomery Flagg. *I Want You for U.S. Army*. Poster, 1917. (Permission Trustees of the Imperial War Museum, London.)

Research has shown that the blind often do develop their other senses to compensate for lack of vision, sometimes to an astounding degree. Run your finger over a line of Braille type, and you will be astonished to find how underdeveloped your sense of touch is. H. G. Wells used the "sixth sense" of the blind as the basis for an intriguing story, *The Country of the Blind*. A sighted man wanders into a village where the inhabitants have been blind for fifteen generations and finds himself severely handicapped in dealing with these strange people whose whole way of life is structured around the use of other senses.

WHY THE EYE?

The detection of light and shadow is essential to the survival of most forms of life. Plants depend on light; even some one-celled animals have light-detecting areas. The simple ability to detect the presence or absence of light can be enough to warn of an approaching enemy. Some curious and ingenious structures have evolved in lower animals. The compound eye of the fly, for example, is made up of thousands of separate lenses, each set at a different angle, which enable it to detect movement from almost any direction. This is why flies are so successful at eluding flyswatters! Snails carry their eyes on the tips of movable antenna-like structures. Chameleons and other reptiles can move each eye separately and rotate them almost three hundred sixty degrees. Birds' eyes look to the side, which is why the pigeon in the park must cock his head to look at something. Many night-hunting animals have vertical pupils that close off surrounding images and zero in on the prey. The victims of such hunters often have horizontal pupils, giving them a wider range of vision more suited to vigilance than to attack. Specialized vision occurs throughout the animal kingdom: visual structures and systems have developed according to specific needs. Selective vision detects only those things necessary for survival. Wasted effort is eliminated.

Human vision is no different. We have to perceive and interpret our environment in complex ways. Blindness is probably the single most severe handicap that a person can suffer. Even moderate flaws in vision interfere with normal functioning in everyday life and are considered serious enough to be corrected. Moreover, our eyes represent more to us than a mere mechanical device for catching light waves from the environment. For most people the experience of seeing represents an ultimate proof: *I saw it with my own eyes!* When we are forced to doubt our eyes we are most uncomfortable, for we depend on them to tell us the truth. But just exactly how reliable are they?

THE HUMAN EYE

We are surrounded by wavelengths of energy called *electromagnetic radiation*, but the human eye can detect only one octave out of a total of at least sixty known octaves of radiation (Figure 2-4).

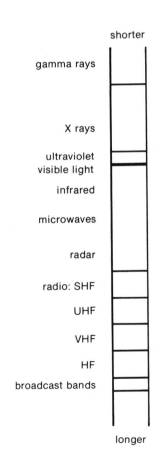

shorter

gamma rays

X rays

ultraviolet
visible light

infrared

microwaves

radar

radio: SHF

UHF

VHF

HF

broadcast bands

longer

2-4. The electromagnetic spectrum.

Just as there are sounds you cannot hear, there is light you cannot see. We are familiar with some of these invisible wavelengths through receivers other than the eye: X rays, gamma rays, ultraviolet rays, infrared rays, microwaves, radio waves. Although we can see only a very limited range of the radiation around us, evolutionary development has made us sensitive to the narrow range most useful to our survival. Human vision, then, is selective at the very start. And it continues to be selective at every single step along the pathway of perception.

THE EYEBALL
The human eyeball is shaped like a sphere and is about an inch in diameter. It is set into a rigid, bony socket so that only the front surface is exposed. Most of the eyeball is covered by a tough white layer (*sclera*), commonly called the white of the eye.

The eyelashes filter out foreign matter but allow light through. You automatically use this protective filter when you squint in a cloud of blowing dust. Eyebrows, together with the overhang of the forehead, provide a built-in sunshade and protect the eyes from falling objects such as raindrops and insects.

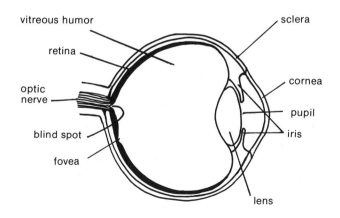

2-5. Cross section of the human eyeball.

The eyeball is kept moist by the secretion of salty tears, which also act as a mild disinfectant. The flow of tears is stimulated by irritants such as smoke, chemicals, and strong wind, as well as by intense emotion. Blinking keeps the eye surface lubricated and washes out foreign matter. You are momentarily blind during a blink. When something happens too rapidly to see, you may say it happened in the wink of an eye.

THE CORNEA
Bulging out from the surface of the eyeball is a tough, transparent, protective layer called the *cornea*. To feel the shape of your cornea, close your eyes and move them while gently touching your eyelid. You can see someone else's cornea by looking at the eye from the side. The cornea bends light rays inward, gathering them together in an area small enough to enter the eyeball. To accomplish this accurately, the surface of the cornea must be smoothly curved. Irregularities in the cornea (*astigmatism*) cause distortions in vision, which can be corrected by eyeglasses or contact lenses.

THE IRIS
Behind the cornea is the *iris*, which gives the eye its color. Color in the iris is caused by distribution of a pigment called *melanin*, which is also present in skin and causes shades of skin color and freckles. The iris is similar in function to the diaphragm of a camera: it is a circular muscle, which expands or contracts to control the amount of light entering the eyeball.

The pupil is the round opening in the center of the iris, and it varies in size as the iris expands or contracts. When you are in a dark room and turn on a lamp, the iris contracts to screen out some of the light, and your pupils become smaller. When you enter a darkened place such as a movie theatre, the iris opens up to allow more light to enter the eye, and your pupils enlarge. Certain drugs and medicines also influence the functioning of the iris. Heroin and other opiates constrict the pupils, while amphetamines enlarge them. Special medications are sometimes used to expand (*dilate*) the pupils during an eye examination.

The iris is affected by emotion: it may expand slightly when you look at something highly desirable or when you concentrate. Ancient oriental jade dealers are said to have carefully watched the pupils of their customers. When the buyer saw a piece of jade that he really wanted, his pupils would widen slightly, even though he might be careful to show no outward sign. The jade dealer then knew which piece the buyer coveted and could quote a high price for it. Recent experiments have shown that the pupils of male subjects tend to widen when they look at a picture of an attractive female in a bikini. We cannot control the functioning of the iris: it is fully automatic.

THE CRYSTALLINE LENS

Behind the iris is the *crystalline lens*. It concentrates the light directed from the cornea and bends the light rays to converge on a small spot within the eyeball. The lens is somewhat elastic: it can flatten slightly or bulge to become more round so you can focus on objects at different distances (*accommodation*). The lens' ability to accommodate lessens with age. A young child can focus on an object as close as four inches from his eyes, a young adult may require ten inches, and an aging person sixteen.

The greatest single cause of blindness is the development of opaqueness within the lens (*cataract*). The pupil of a person with a cataract looks gray or silvery. Aging increases the possibility of cataracts, but they can also be caused by diabetes or excessive radiation. Blindness caused by cataracts is dramatically cured by surgery that removes the lens completely! The patient must then wear thick glasses as a substitute.

THE VITREOUS HUMOR

The main cavity of the eyeball is filled with a clear, jellylike substance called the *vitreous humor* or *vitreous body*. Light waves travel through this substance on their way to the retina. Normally the vitreous humor is clear, but sometimes small particles such as red corpuscles may become trapped in it. These appear as tiny dots or gray filaments, which are called *floaters*. You can see them if you look at something featureless like a blank white wall or a blue sky. You cannot focus on them: if you try, they seem to drift away.

THE RETINA

About four-fifths of the inside of the eyeball is covered by several layers of cells about the thickness of a postage stamp: the *retina*. The retina is an arrangement of light-sensitive cells (*photoreceptors*). Like a switch which must be either on or off, each photoreceptor is capable of only two states: stimulated or not stimulated. Light reaching a camera's film records an image, but light entering the eyeball can only trigger a pattern of on/off photoreceptor activity, much like a two-dimensional mosaic pattern. Despite this astounding limitation on input, you are able to experience depth, motion, size, shape, texture, and position, as well as to make all manner of inferences about the nature of what you see!

One reason you perceive as much visual information as you do is because of the very small size of the photoreceptors. The problem is rather like trying to create a picture with a mosaic pattern of dots—as is sometimes done in newspaper photographs. If you use large dots, you cannot accumulate much detail in the image, but if you use very small dot units, you can express greater detail—the smaller the dots, the more detail you can define (Figure 2-6). The units used to build the mosaic pattern in the human eye are the size of the cells themselves. The smallest photoreceptor is one micron (one-millionth of a meter), or .00003937 inch! The number of cells on a *single* retina is over two hundred million—more than the entire population of the United States! In addition, the sensitivity of the photoreceptors is so acute that they can be stimulated by a single quantum—the smallest amount of radiant energy that exists!

The photoreceptors in the retina are normally stimulated or turned on by light, but they may be stimulated by other means as well. For example, if you simply close your eyes hard or rub them, you can "see" flashes of light (*phosphenes*), which result from turning on the retinal cells by pressure. Some drugs and physiological conditions (migraine headaches, epilepsy) can also stimulate visual sensations related to sensations of light. Stimulation of the retinal cells from *any* source is transmitted to the brain as *light*.

Look steadily at the black square in Figure 2-7 for at least sixty seconds in good light, then look at the blank area on the right. The glowing white square that you "see" is called an *afterimage*—an image remaining after actual visual contact is over. If you look at Figure 2-8 for several seconds, white As it fades, blinking may bring it back. The afterimage in this case is a negative one, for it appears in opposite colors to the original stimulus. Negative afterimages occur with colored stimuli, too (see Chapter 8). Afterimages are experienced after prolonged or intense exposure to a stimulus, during the interval when the retinal cells are returning to their normal state. They are common occurrences,

but you normally tune them out. Occasionally an afterimage is so intense that it actually interferes with vision—for example, when you have your picture taken with a flashbulb. The cause of the afterimage phenomenon has been attributed by various investigators to adaptation, fatigue, saturation, or bleaching of the photoreceptors in the retina.

Some optical artists have used the afterimage response to generate visual activity in the viewer. If you look at Figure 2-8 for several seconds, white circles will begin to dance among the black ones. A related phenomenon appears in simple grid figures. Look at the black squares in Figure 2-9. Can you see gray spots at the intersections of the white spaces? Try to look directly at one of them. What happens?

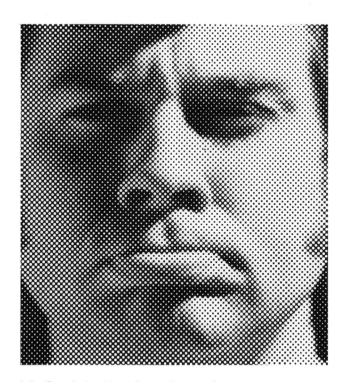

2-6. (Permission Mead Paper, Dayton, Ohio.)

2-7.

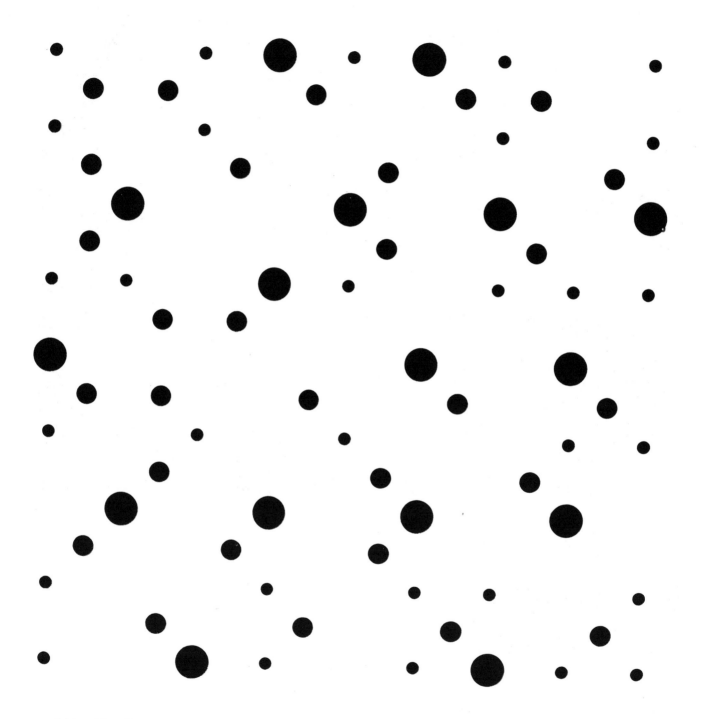

2-8. Bridget Riley. *Fragment No. 6*. Plexiglass print, 29¼ by 29 inches, 1965. (Permission Galerie Denise René, Paris.)

2-9.

One small area on the back of the retina, the *blind spot*, contains no photoreceptors. This is the point at which the nerve fibers from the retinal cells gather together to form the optic nerve, which transmits the pattern of cell stimulation to the brain. Normally you are unaware of the blind spot, because the part of the image that falls on the blind spot of one eye does not fall on the blind spot of the other. Also, the blind spot is not located in the central portion of your vision, where you would be more sensitive to it. You can experience your own blind spot by looking at Figure 2-10. Close your left eye and focus your right on the square. Move the book alternately closer and farther away from your eyes. The circle will disappear when its image falls on the blind spot. Reverse the procedure to experience the blind spot in the other eye.

The photoreceptors lining the retina are of two types: *rods* and *cones* (named for their shapes). The cones are activated during daylight and under good light conditions. We perceive color, form, and detail with the cones. The rods are smaller but much more sensitive to light; they function for night vision and in poor illumination. They seem to be more sensitive to motion than to form.

The rods contain a pigment called *visual purple* or *rhodopsin*. This pigment bleaches chemically when it is exposed to light, and it must be reformed in darkness before the rods can function. When you enter a dark room, the iris quickly expands to let in more light, but the formation of visual purple (*dark adaptation*) is not fully completed for several minutes. Vitamin A in the body is used to replace and reform visual purple. A diet deficient in vitamin A for as short a period as a month can result in a significant degree of night blindness.

The rods and cones are not evenly distributed across the retina. The rods are less dense around the center of the retina, whereas the most densely packed area of cones (*fovea*) lies directly behind the lens, and it is here that vision is sharpest. The fovea contains virtually no rods, which means that in night vision it is not very useful. To see something more clearly at night, it is often necessary to look a little to one side so that the image falls outside the foveal area onto the rods. This technique is well known to astronomers and sailors, who depend on night-vision skills.

2-10.

Although the point of focus is normally on the fovea, light also stimulates photoreceptors on surrounding areas in the retina (*peripheral vision*). This is why, even when you are looking directly at something, you are also aware of its surroundings. In your peripheral vision you are more aware of generalized shapes and forms than of small details. Peripheral vision is particularly sensitive to motion. This ability to see out of the corner of the eye is very important, particularly in driving. People who have lost their peripheral vision are said to have *tunnel vision*, which means that they can see only straight ahead. You can test your peripheral vision by looking straight ahead and slowly moving your fingers to the side out of your range of vision. Just at the point when you can no longer see them, move them slightly. You will find that you can see the fingers at the very edge of your visual field when they are in motion, although you cannot see them when they are still!

EYE MOVEMENTS

Even without moving your head, you can quickly and easily move your eyes across a wide field of vision. This is possible because three pairs of muscles move each eyeball: one pair moves it to the right or left, another pair turns it up or down, and the third pair rotates it (Figure 2-11). The muscles in both eyes must move in unison, since it is important for the image to fall on corresponding parts of each retina. Defective eye-muscle coordination can cause vision problems such as cross-eyes (turned toward each other), walleyes (turned away from each other), or amblyopia (lazy eye). Unless these problems are corrected by exercise or lenses, they may cause double vision or other difficulties.

Your eyes make several basic types of movements. You make smooth motions or slow drifts when you are keeping a moving object in sight by moving either your eyes or your head. Fast jumps occur when you move your eyes from one fixed point to another, as when you read, look at a painting, or scan a landscape. Some speed-reading techniques train the reader to spend less time on each fixation and to decrease the total number of fixations. While the eyes are actually moving, they can register only a blur, since the visual field is sweeping across the retina at a rapid rate. You make eye-fixation movements when you look at a work of art. This is why the scale or size of an artwork is such an important factor in the experience of seeing it. It takes many fixations across a broad area to see and assimilate a large painting or sculpture, but when you look at a small work or a reproduction in a book, the total can often be seen with one fixation. Many modern artists produce very large-scale works. This requires more visual involvement by the viewer and gives a new kind of visual experience to someone used to smaller works. This is one reason why looking at a reproduction in a book is never a substitute for the experience of seeing an original work of art.

During the early stages of sleep the eyes make slow, rolling motions; during periods of dreaming rapid eye movements (REMs) occur that are similar to the scanning movements of waking. The sleeper seems to be watching a movie behind his eyelids. With patience you can observe these eye movements in another person while he is sleeping. If you dare, wake the person during a REM period. He is almost certain to be dreaming vividly and to be able to recall the dream. If he is left asleep, however, he will probably have forgotten the dream by morning.

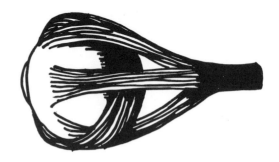

2-11. Eye muscles.

Another type of eye movement consists of rapid oscillations or tremors, which occur at a frequency of thirty to seventy per second. These constant movements are necessary for normal vision, because an image fixed on the same cells would fade after a few seconds. Try staring at a small speck on a blank surface without allowing your eyes to move. The speck will alternately appear and disappear because of this saturation effect in the retinal cells. Rapid, small motions shift the image onto different receptors, thereby constantly stimulating new ones and compensating for the fading effect.

The shimmering or vibrating effects of some simple repeating patterns (Figure 2-12) may be due in part to these rapid oscillations, possibly in combination with afterimage and border-contrast effects. Some optical artists have made use of this phenomenon to create works of art that seem to shimmer and vibrate (Figure 2-13).

The process of human vision is highly selective, even within the eye. Because of its structure your eye can receive and react only to certain types of information. The light rays that finally reach the retina provide the basis for all your visual experiences of depth, motion, size, shape, texture, and position. Your inferences about reality and the nature of your world are based on the transformation of light waves within a delicate and complex structure in which all parts must work in harmony—a structure in which even a small malfunction may wreak havoc with the whole. That you negotiate daily through the physical world seems somewhat of a miracle when you consider how severely your input is limited by the eye, even before it can reach the next processing level—the brain.

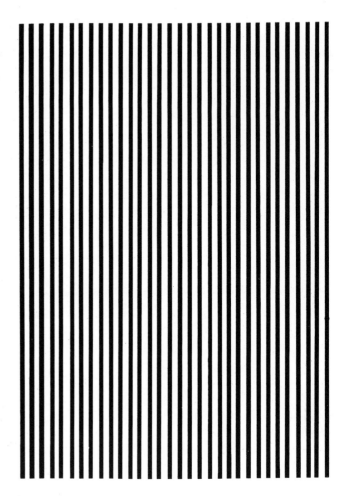

2-12. Don't use this for wallpaper!

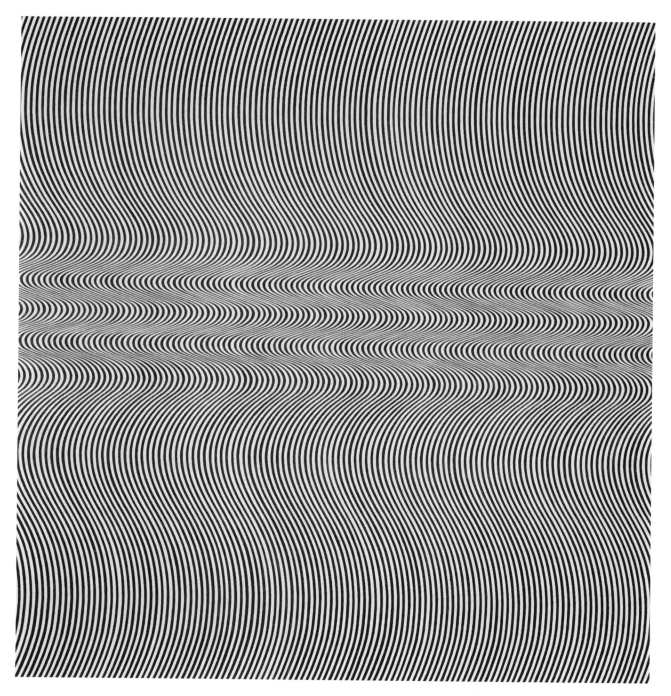

2-13. Bridget Riley. *Current.* Synthetic emulsion on composition
board, 58⅜ by 58⅞ inches, 1964. (Collection The Museum of
Modern Art, New York. Phillip Johnson Fund.)

3. THE BRAIN:

It Figures

Look carefully at Figure 3-1. Look for a figure like ⚹ . Can you see it? Now, look again for another identical figure formed by the spaces *between* the original figure. Practice looking alternately at each figure. Do the wedges that form each one seem to stand out and even to be brighter than the background wedges? Can you experience the difference between seeing the drawing as lines and seeing it as shapes? As you concentrate on these different ways of seeing, the drawing seems to subtly change—even though *no change occurs on the page!* Why?

This simple experiment shows how very easily the brain transforms and organizes information from the retina: the retinal image does not change, yet your perceptions *do* change. Seeing is accomplished not in the eye—but in the mind.

Little is known about the exact process by which the brain converts energy into perceptual experience. We do know that cells in the brain accept and process input from the eye by means of electrical and chemical activity. Evidence indicates that perceptions, memories, and "mental images" result from coded combinations of electrochemical activity among brain cells. Because of this the brain is sometimes described as a kind of computer—although no computer yet invented is capable of a fraction of the complex processing that occurs in the simplest of human perceptions.

For one thing the sheer number of brain cells is staggering. If people were scaled down to the size of brain cells, "we could hold the population of the earth in our cupped hands, but there would not be enough people to make one brain."[1]

Research data reveals complex, intimate, and mysterious relationships between eye and brain, showing that these two organs are linked in profound ways. Things happening in or to the eye (blindness, eye position, exposure to color) affect the electrical rhythms of the brain, sometimes to a great extent. Conversely, electrode stimulation from inside the brain can cause people to "see" flashes of light or complete vivid scenes and to experience elaborate visual memories. Other more common internal events also cause visual sensations.

3-1.

Increased blood pressure in the brain, as in a migraine headache, can cause visual disturbances such as flashes, distortions, or spots. Abnormal electrical activity in the brain of an epileptic may cause him to experience sensations of light, noise, taste, or smell. Mild drugs and narcotics such as marijuana and alcohol can heighten or depress perception of external reality. More intense chemical stimulation of the brain with stronger drugs such as LSD and mescaline may create visual experiences completely unrelated to external events and of such an intensity that the individual cannot distinguish them from outside reality (*hallucinations*).

Even such a simple thing as lack of sleep, if it is carried to an extreme, may generate grotesque imagery much like a drug user's "bad trip." Experimental subjects deprived of sleep for thirty to sixty hours experience changes in size and depth perception, as well as illusions of movement and halo effects around lights. By the time the subjects have gone without sleep for ninety hours, they lose their sense of time and often have full-blown hallucinations. Disc jockeys and other people who have tried to set "wakethon" records exhibit the same pattern.

Some researchers have been interested in finding out what happens to people in the opposite situation—totally deprived of outside stimulation. The subject is isolated in a cubicle, his eyes and ears are covered to shut out sight and sound, his hands are heavily gloved to restrict his sense of touch, and a continuously running machine provides a noise cover. Under these conditions the brain's activity depends on whatever stimulation and meaning it can create for itself and by itself. Subjects report that their minds begin to drift after a while; they become unable to concentrate on any thoughts; they have visual and auditory hallucinations that they cannot control; sometimes they develop paranoia about the experiment; they feel an increasingly desperate and unpleasant urgency for any kind of outside stimulation. Negative effects on vision, thinking, and feelings persist for days after the end of the experiment (Figure 3-2). Small wonder that brainwashing victims undergo drastic conversions or that solitary confinement is so universally feared!

It is worth noting that these delusions, hallucinations, and other brain, motor, and psychological disturbances are strikingly similar for sleep-deprived and sensory-deprived subjects. Both prolonged over- and understimulation seem to negatively affect the brain and vision in similar ways. Interestingly enough, however, Zen devotees and yogis can meditate uninterruptedly for as long as five days without exhibiting the distortions and confusions that occur in normal subjects who are sense- or sleep-deprived for the same periods of time. Many questions about states of consciousness and the rhythms of brain activity remain to be answered.

3-2. Sensory-deprivation subject. After four days of deprivation, he could not hold a rod in a hole without hitting the sides. (Yale Joel, Time-Life Picture Agency © Time, Inc.)

Experiments with the electricity and chemistry of the brain have led some imaginative observers to fantasize that an art form of the future could be based on experiential packages, in which the aesthetic experience would be created by electronic brain inputs or drugs. The electronic or chemical "artist" would design and program drug capsules or electrical inputs as "works of art."[2]

Although we know little about exactly *how* the brain works, we can make many observations about *what* the brain does to create meaning from the jumble of data transmitted to it from the eye.

IMAGE FUSION

A fundamental phenomenon of human vision is that the brain fuses two retinal images into a single image. Normally, you accomplish the fusion of images easily and unconsciously, because even though each eye sees a slightly different image (*disparity*), the images are very similar, and they overlap each other. Your brain will go to great lengths to maintain the perception of a single image—even when the result defies common sense. Two simple experiments will demonstrate this. For the first one you need a tube about the size and length of a paper-towel tube; you can make one by rolling up an ordinary sheet of paper lengthwise. Keep both eyes open and hold the tube up to your right eye with your right hand. Slowly move the open palm of your left hand toward the tube until it touches the outside of the tube near the end (Figure 3-3). What do you see?

3-3.

You may have done the second experiment when you were a child. Simply focus on something straight ahead of you several feet away. Keep that focus and point the tips of your index fingers toward each other until they touch. You will see what looks like a small segment of a double-nailed finger held in place by your two index fingers. By moving your hands closer to and further away from your eyes—still keeping the initial focal point—you will see this "phantom finger" grow and shrink in size.

Even more bizarre effects occur when the image shown to each eye is markedly different. As the brain attempts to form a solid, single image, it may alternately accept and reject parts of the image from each eye. When colors provide the stimulus, the observer may see first one color, then the other rather than a mixture of the two. With patterns or pictures different parts phase in and out, combining and recombining in various and constantly changing ways. This phenomenon is called *retinal* or *binocular rivalry*. It suggests that the brain sometimes has trouble choosing between two competing images; following King Solomon's famous suggestion, it divides the child.

TUNEOUT

Both animals and humans will stop reacting to a stimulus when it is repeated again and again. The *constant* aspects of a situation seem to vanish from your consciousness. You tune out the constant hums and noises of clocks, heating systems, and appliances. You tune out the rhythm of your breathing, the beating of your heart, the feel of clothing against your skin, the temperature of the air. Adaptation to these constant factors causes you to ignore them. Although such stimuli are not consciously perceived, experimental data indicates that the nervous system nevertheless continues to register them. And if such stimuli are removed or undergo some change (a heart palpitation, a cold draft, a sudden silence), you are instantly alert.

Because of the tendency to tune them out, the most constant elements are sometimes the hardest to perceive. You may think your water has no taste—until you drink water from someplace else.

City nights may seem relatively quiet—until you try to sleep in the silence of the country. You may be unaware of gradually increasing darkness—until someone turns on a light. Tuning out keeps you from directing conscious attention to factors in your environment that are not apt to provide you with new information. This basic selective process keeps you focused on only as much of a given situation as necessary. You are spared the burden of *overload*, the result of reacting to too many things at once.

But this protective principle has disadvantages as well. Worker tuneout in repetitive industrial assembly-line tasks can lead to accidents and production errors. Tuneout from the constant monotony of turnpike driving is also dangerous. The first, arrow-straight turnpikes were technologically efficient, but they did not take into account the human factor, and high accident rates resulted. Designers of superhighways now consciously plan curves and rough-pavement approaches to toll booths; these stimuli help to keep drivers alert.

Sleep is the tuneout par excellence, for in sleep we banish all sensory stimuli from consciousness for hours at a time. Many people can sleep through incredible noises without waking. In certain stages of sleep the sleeper remains "blind" to the outside world, even when his eyes are opened and a light is shone into them! No wonder many cultures associate sleep with the absence of the soul or with death. Consider the familiar prayer, "Now I lay me down to sleep . . ."

FIGURE/GROUND

With the constant aspects of a situation tuned out, you are free to direct your attention to things that are more likely to involve new information. The constant factors become a background for things of more immediate meaning. One of the first decisions your mind makes is to select what to tune out and what to tune in. Your mind often makes such decisions automatically and without your conscious control.

Look at Figure 3-4a: a cross against the background of the paper. Even with a square around it (Figure 3-4b), the cross and not the surrounding space remains the meaningful part of this simple stimulus. The Gestalt psychologists called the relationship between a figure and its background the *figure/ground relationship*. Figure 3-1 is an experiment in the conscious alternation of figure/ground relationships.

Certain characteristics consistently accompany the perception of figures. A figure is perceptually *bright:* it is seen with more intensity and as standing out from the background. That is why the wedges you concentrate on in Figure 3-1 seem brighter than the other wedges. A figure also has the quality of being a *thing* and of being *on top of* the background. The ground also has specific characteristics: it seems to be *behind* the figure, to lack a particular form, and to be *continuous*—that is, you do not perceive it as stopping at the edge of the figure but rather as going on behind the figure. A figure suggests meaning, while a ground seems relatively meaningless.

The formation of figure/ground relationships is the most essential operation in perception. It takes place with all the senses. At this very moment you can become aware of your consciousness forming figures. Pause in your reading and concentrate for a moment on your body. You may become aware of your position and change it. You may feel an itch and decide to scratch it (notice the power of suggestion!). You might become aware of a taste in your mouth and decide to take a break and get a drink of water. You may become aware of sounds: a radio or TV, a passing automobile, a dog barking. Many things will emerge as perceptual figures that until now were parts of the background.

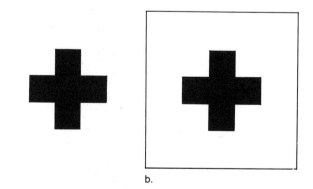

a. b.

3-4.

Normally, your mind exerts an incredible amount of selectivity on the sensations coming in from all your senses. You cannot maintain anything like the objectivity of a machine. That is why it is so often surprising to play back a tape recording: the amount of background noise is astonishing. A microphone has no ability to form figure/ground relationships—it picks up everything indiscriminately. The recording shows you how much you tuned out. A camera does the same thing. Have you ever been surprised at how messy the surroundings appear in a snapshot? You can be so busy concentrating on the subject of the photograph that you tune out the visual impact of the background. In order to "see what the camera sees," professional photographers must overcome this natural tendency to tune out background factors.

Figure/ground relationships do not exist in the outside world but are created by the mind's selective organization. A figure in one situation can become the ground in another. If you are looking at a painting—say, a portrait—you first perceive the face as a figure. But as you look at it, you begin to notice certain details—perhaps the eyes. As you concentrate on the eyes, they become a figure and the face recedes into ground. The entire painting can become a figure seen against the ground of the wall. Something is a figure when you pay attention to it; at that particular moment all else drops away to become a background.

Sometimes things become figures against your will—for example, the ticking of a clock. Ordinarily such a constant noise stays in your auditory background. But you may suddenly become aware of it—probably just when you are trying to fall asleep. It may remain as a figure with annoying persistence; you'd like to push it back into the background, yet you can't. The same sort of thing may happen when you are feeling irritable. If you have a headache, even the normal background noise of a household can become impossible to ignore. Everything becomes an annoyance. Painkillers, tranquilizers, and other drugs are used to push pain or problems into the background and to generate a pleasant figure (or no figure) in place of an unpleasant one.

Many encounter-group activities, consciousness-raising methods, and self-awareness techniques are designed to make people aware of background factors that they ordinarily tune out. These activities help people to form new figure/ground relationships and thereby to perceive themselves and others with new awareness. Gestalt therapy in particular sensitizes people to emotional figure/ground relationships within the personality. Meditation, another technique, is directed toward disengaging the self from certain kinds of figures in order to achieve a state of integrated unity.

ALTERNATING FIGURE/GROUND

Sometimes figure and ground seem to vacillate between two equally good alternatives. As you look at the well-known Peter and Paul goblet (Figure 3-5), notice how the qualities of black and white change with each view, alternately showing the perceptual characteristics of figure and ground. When you look at the goblet, it seems to stand out, and the black seems like a continuous space behind it. When you look at the faces, the white seems to recede, and the black to stand out.

3-5.

Psychologists generally agree that both views cannot be perceived simultaneously. That is, although you see different meanings (*ambiguity*) in turn, at any given instant you can see only one meaning. This suggests important limits on the number of stimuli to which you can attend at any given time. The experience of ambiguity results from an inability to stabilize one meaning as preferable to the other.

At first thought it might seem as if a figure and its ground ought to mirror each other in shape, but this doesn't hold true. Concentrate on the black area in Figure 3-6 as the figure, with the white as the space into which it is projecting. Then reverse your perception and study the white shape against the black background. The shapes are surprisingly different in character. You encounter this phenomenon when jigsaw-puzzle pieces do not look like the spaces into which they fit.

Artists use alternating figure/ground possibilities to a large extent—sometimes obviously, sometimes subtly. Look at Figures 3-7, 3-8, 3-9, and 3-10. You can consciously exercise your ability to alternate figure and ground with each one.

3-7. An American patchwork-quilt pattern: *Melon Patch*.

3-6.

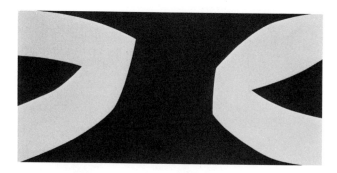

3-8. Ellsworth Kelly. *East River*. Oil on canvas, 47⅛ by 100⅛ inches, 1963. (Courtesy The Art Institute of Chicago.)

3-9. M. C. Escher. *Circle Limit IV (Heaven and Hell)*. Woodcut, 16 inches in diameter, 1960. (Permission Escher Foundation, Haags Gemeentemuseum, The Hague.)

The experience of ambiguity bothers many people. In our culture figure has always been accorded major importance, while ground has been defined as those factors that can be eliminated without affecting meaning. Eastern thought, on the other hand, recognizes that one cannot exist without the other. The yin/yang symbol (Figure 3-11) expresses the basic Chinese concept that figure and ground are inextricably bound together: the form of one determines the form of the other. Due to this concept, oriental thought is characterized by an ability to tolerate conflict and paradox. In this sense it embraces the dynamic duality of perceptual organization. Oriental art reflects this point of view, and it has always placed great value on the use of empty space to represent meaningful parts of a picture. The Japanese screen painting (Figure 3-12) shows one historical style that uses enigmatic blank spaces. From one point of view they seem like holes or interruptions behind the picture, but from another they are like opaque clouds in front of the scene. Because the houses and people are more meaningful figures, your mind tends to want them in front of, not behind, the blank spaces. The alternation and conflict actively engage your perceptual judgment.

3-10. (Photograph by Bruce Thompson, 1972.)

3-11.

3-12. Unidentified Japanese Artist. *Battles between the Genji and the Heike* (detail from a pair of six-fold screens). Color and gold on paper, late sixteenth century. (Permission Metropolitan Museum of Art, New York, Rogers Fund.)

3-13. (Photograph by Bruce Thompson.)

GROUPING

An interruption of the image also takes place in high-contrast photography (Figure 3-13), which reduces an image to black and white and thereby eliminates the outside contours and degrees of shading that we ordinarily expect to find. The fact that you can organize images so easily from such fragments emphasizes how readily your mind works to fill in the blanks. This can be carried to a high level of gamesmanship (Figure 3-14). Whether or not you can see this image depends upon your ability to form figure/ground relationships from seemingly random, black-and-white shapes. But some people have claimed that only true believers can see the figure of Jesus!

Zen painters achieve something similar by an emphasis on minimal brush strokes to convey a meaningful image. Paintings such as the one shown in Figure 3-15 are composed of fragments—brush strokes mostly meaningless in themselves but combined by the mind of the viewer into a definite image.

3-14. Source unknown.

3-15. Kimura Nagamitsu. *Figures and Landscape*. Kano period. (Courtesy Museum of Fine Arts, Boston.)

Grouping is one way your mind perceptually organizes a figure/ground relationship from separate elements. In the examples we have considered so far this strategy was rewarded by closure with a meaningful figure. Some elements, however, cannot be organized into a single meaningful figure. This is particularly true of overall patterns made up of many identical or nearly identical units. As you look at Figure 3-16, interesting things happen. The triangles group and regroup themselves. Some seem lighter than others, even though they are all equally black. Strong diagonal groupings may form. You might suddenly see a lattice structure of square boxes, with the black triangles forming shadows. Many perceptual organizations occur as your mind persists in trying to arrive at permanent closure. The effort is doomed, because the visual stimulus lends itself equally well to different possibilities. Some optical artists have made skillful use of this phenomenon (Figure 3-17).

3-16.

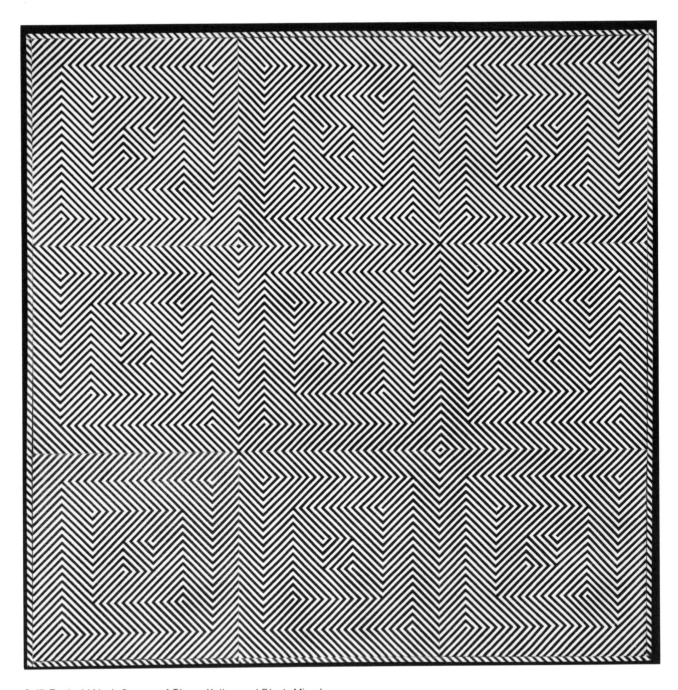

3-17. Reginald Neal. *Square of Three, Yellow and Black.* Mixed
media, 32 by 32 inches, 1964. (Permission New Jersey State
Museum.)

Visual structures of this sort, composed of repeated patterns of identical or nearly identical elements, are called *periodic structures*. Elements in the pattern occur *periodically*, that is, at regular and predictable intervals. Surprising things happen when two or more periodic patterns are superimposed on one another. Additional patterns are organized by the mind from the points at which the patterns intersect. Figure 3-18 consists of three straight-line grids. Notice how circular patterns emerge from the network of straight lines!

The intersecting points of lines may seem blacker than they really are (Figure 3-19). If the angle of intersection is less than thirty degrees, the pattern forms a *moiré*. This French word originally referred to a fabric made from two layers of finely striated silk pressed onto each other slightly out of alignment, resulting in a characteristic shimmering surface. The Fresnel-Ring moiré (Figure 3-20) is formed from a set of parallel lines combined with one set of concentric circles.

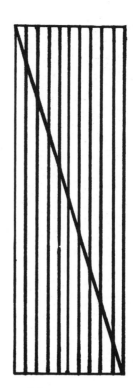

3-19. Single-line moiré.

3-20. Fresnel-Ring moiré.

3-18.

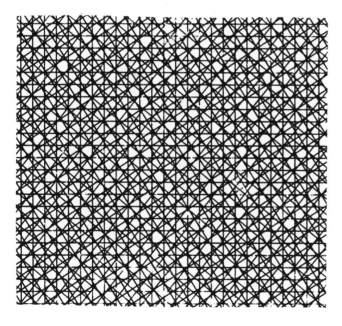

You can also see moiré patterns by looking through the folds of thin curtains or the overlapping centers of adjustable window screens, and they may be observed among the wires of suspension bridges and in the finely engraved lines of stamps or money. Superimposed sound frequencies also create new patterns. When two tones of differing frequency are played together, a third, throbbing sound is formed by the instants when the peaks and troughs of the sound waves coincide. In all these cases the mind forms new figures from points at which elements in two or more patterns intersect.

ALTERNATING FIGURES

We have been concerned up to now with the mind's search to establish a figure. But sometimes seeing a figure only begins a new set of perceptual problems. Each drawing in Figure 3-21 confronts you with a figure that alternates between two or more equally good interpretations. A certain tension results and, like a caged animal, your mind carries out a repetitive pattern: it goes endlessly back and forth between possible meanings, unable to confirm one view as more correct than another.

3-21.

Look at Figure 3-22. Do you see a young woman looking away from you? Or do you see a toothless old crone whose chin is turned down into her fur collar? If you can't see both, keep looking. The second face will usually appear quite suddenly. Unless you are familiar with this drawing or are just naturally suspicious, you probably would have been satisfied with your first interpretation. Your mind tends to see only what is necessary for meaning.

Once you have made closure, you do not usually expect further information to be forthcoming. Mystery writers such as Agatha Christie and Arthur Conan Doyle exploit the closure process by constructing a story in such a way that the reader forms "false" figures, while important clues are tuned out. The detective's skill lies in seeing figures that others have not seen. With one masterful stroke the significance of many details changes, and a new figure—the solution—emerges.

Figures 3-23, 3-24, and 3-25 show how some artists have used the phenomenon of alternating figures. In each picture visual evidence is given for more than one view, and your mind is unable to confirm one as more correct than another.

3-22. The wife and the mother-in-law.

3-23. Jasper Johns. *0-9*. Lithograph, 1960. (Collection The
Museum of Modern Art, New York. Gift of Mr. and Mrs. Arnold
P. Bartos.)

3-24. Josef Albers. *JHC II.* Engraving on plastic, 20 by 26 inches,
1963. (Permission Mr. and Mrs. James H. Clark, Dallas.)

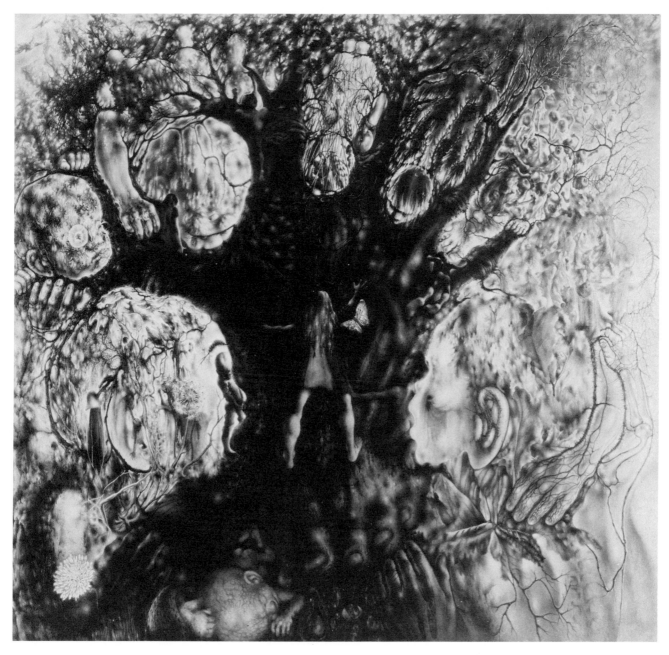

3-25. Pavel Tchelitchew. *Hide and Seek.* Oil, 74½ by 84¾ inches, 1940–1942. (Collection The Museum of Modern Art, New York. Mrs. Simon Guggenheim Fund.)

EXAGGERATION

Figures 3-26, 3-27, and 3-28 show familiar optical illusions. Differing theories account for their effectiveness, but some evidence suggests that once your mind has perceived certain characteristics in a stimulus, it goes one step further and perceives these characteristics as existing to an even greater extent than they actually do. "Pride goeth before a fall"—and here the mind seems to suffer the consequences of overconfidence about the closure it has made.

According to this theory, when two patterns are seen together, perception of the weaker pattern is distorted in order to maintain an exaggerated perception of the stronger one. In Figure 3-26 actual line length, a weaker aspect of the stimulus, is overpowered by a directional response to the angular lines at the ends. The radiating lines of Figure 3-27 provide the stronger pattern and are seen as having more spread than they actually do; to maintain this percept, the mind must distort the parallel lines. In Figure 3-28 the short cross-hatches dominate the perception of a parallel relationship between the vertical lines. Such exaggerations seem to be largely beyond conscious control.

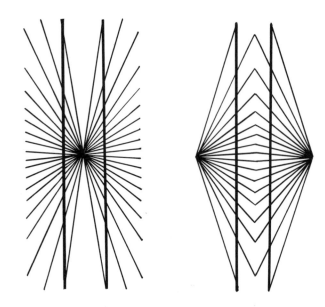

3-27. The Hering figure, or fan illusion.

3-28. Herringbone illusion.

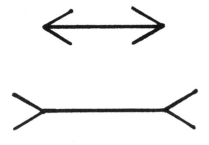

3-26. Muller-Lyer arrow illusion.

PREPATTERNING

So far we have examined the mind's strategies for selecting and organizing stimuli. These strategies are all directed toward one goal: to make meaning out of a jumble of sensory data and arrive at closure. But why does closure occur? What is there in the mind that says, "OK, you can stop now—it computes!"

The early Gestalt psychologists thought that characteristics inherent in the stimulus imposed certain closure patterns on the mind. Current research in perception, however, tends to shift emphasis from the structure of the stimulus to the structure of the mind itself. According to this newer view, closure demonstrates the reverse: that *the mind has succeeded in imposing a pattern on the stimulus.* In other words the stimulus does not determine the closure: instead, a preexisting mental category programs how the stimulus will be perceived.

At first glance this may seem to be a replay of that old game, "Which came first: the chicken or the egg?" But in fact, this new argument has far-reaching implications for understanding human perception. If such a view is correct, your mind does not interpret stimuli with anything like an open-minded approach. Instead, you can see things only in relation to categories *already established* in your mind. Closure does not represent objective knowledge about a stimulus but rather the *confirmation* of a preexistent idea. It means that on a perceptual level our minds are made up before the fact: we have the closure programmed before the stimulus happens!

Strong evidence supports this view. You are familiar with the Gestalt principle that the mind tends to correct a stimulus to fit the best or simplest interpretation and that the mind tends to see the stimulus as more correct than it actually is (Chapter 1). You are aware of difficulties in proof-reading and similar situations. A good explanation for such mental correcting is provided by postulating that the mind bends and distorts the perception of the stimulus in order to satisfactorily classify or fit it into an already established category. To see the stimulus as a familiar gestalt is easier than to construct a new category to

account for all the minute details that make the present stimulus different from similar stimuli encountered in the past. Notice that this is also consistent with the law of simplicity.

We can call these preprogrammed responses *perceptual prejudices.* As with other kinds of prejudice, it means that you meet a stimulus with a preexisting stereotype, and you tend to see only those things that reinforce it—you tune out other things that are not consistent with it. Some such preprogramming is quite necessary. You could not negotiate through a single day if you had to pay full attention to every stimulus as if you were seeing it for the first time. To be efficient and practical, the brain *must* tune out and categorize at very basic levels. The result is that you encounter reality with an enormous number of preconceived notions.

Knowing this, we can begin to appreciate the enormous difficulty of the search for objective knowledge about the world we live in. Probably no group of people has ever placed a higher value on objective observation than have scientists. The very fabric of the scientific method is woven from extreme strategies to ensure freedom from bias. And yet the history of science provides wonderful examples of how difficult it is to see something when you have no prior acquaintance with its structure. For example, scientists of the early 1600s were ignorant of the fact that Saturn is encircled by rings: even Galileo reported that it was a triple object. Early drawings of the planet clearly reveal a struggle to interpret the telescopic image. Users of early microscopes had similar problems determining the nature of the microorganisms they saw. And future space explorations will certainly subject some of our old, familiar images to new, unforeseen reinterpretations!

4. CONSTANCY:

No Matter What Happens, You'll Always Be the Same to Me

When you look at yourself in the mirror, how big are you—in the mirror? Life-size? Since you are a slight distance away, the image in the mirror is probably slightly smaller than life—but how much smaller? You wouldn't believe me if I told you, so go look at yourself in the mirror. Stand your normal distance away, close one eye, and reach out and measure the image in the mirror. An easy way is to place your thumb on the chin and a finger on the hairline (of course, you could do something creative like squirting a shaving-cream outline on the mirror). Look at what you have measured. Quite a shock, isn't it? My own image turns out to be a scant four inches high (the size of a rather large apple)—and I have always been told that I have quite a long face! At this point you might recall that you can see your total height in a three-foot "full-length" mirror. Another interesting experiment is to close one eye, hold your head still, and trace with a marker on a windowpane the outlines of the objects you see. I guarantee you will be incredulous at the results.

The intriguing thing is not simply that the image is smaller and keeps getting smaller as you move away from the mirror (doubling the distance halves the image)—that's not hard to understand. What is more difficult to comprehend is just how very small that image actually is and why you remain so oblivious to this extraordinary shrinkage. What hap-

pens in the mirror and on the windowpane happens all the time. People move toward you and away from you; you move nearer to and further from things; the images expand and shrink. Yet under normal circumstances you have no problem in perceiving things as their normal size. For example, I know that the Volkswagen in my driveway is smaller than my neighbor's Chrysler, even though from my position the VW's image is many times larger. When I see my friend Benjamin a block away, I know that he is still five foot nine and not a midget, in spite of his small image. The information pattern on the retina is telling me one thing (the VW is bigger than the Chrysler, Ben is a midget)—and yet my brain seems to disregard it. Why? The mind is able to maintain *constant* or unchanged perceptions of objects in spite of continual changes and ambiguities in the retinal pattern. This ability is called *constancy*.

SIZE CONSTANCY

Scientists have observed that a change in the size of the retinal image is not perceived as a change in the size of the object, but rather as a change in the distance of the object. This principle is demonstrated in the laboratory by asking a subject in a darkened room to observe an object whose size is gradually increased and decreased. The subject reports that the object seems to be coming to-

50

ward him and going away.

You don't have to be an experimental subject to experience this phenomenon. Recall the overwhelming feeling of drifting through space that is so much a part of movies like *2001: A Space Odyssey* and *Fantastic Voyage*. Things float toward you; you travel past planets; they recede into the distance. One cartoon character throws a ball at another, and the ball seems to come straight toward you, closer and closer. You are watching a flat screen—yet you sit spellbound, feeling as if you are going through blood vessels or whizzing by planets—and all because a film animator has made circles get larger and smaller! Why should your mind interpret size changes this way?

When the retinal image of an object changes, you are confronted with two possible explanations: either the object has actually changed size or its distance from you has changed. To account for the changed image in terms of changes in the object would be very complicated, and in most instances you would be quite unlikely to find that an object had indeed changed size. You learn very early in life that physical objects are likely to remain the same size, whereas viewing distance frequently varies. As a survival strategy it is much more practical to assume that your distance from an object has changed, even though to accomplish this you must tune out and transform certain aspects of the information received in the eye. You must remember, however, that an identical retinal image *can* be produced by different events: for example, an airborne balloon gradually decreasing in size could be either losing air or drifting away. You cannot rely on automatic size/distance perceptions as absolute certainties; they should be thought of as a practical gamble, a gamble in which the probabilities are usually—but not always—on your side.

CONTEXT
The context in which an object is seen exerts the most important influence on your perception of its size. This is demonstrated in some well-known illusions (Figures 4-1 and 4-2). In everyday life you rarely see objects in isolation. People, furniture, automobiles, trees, houses—all are seen in relation to one another. Size relationships among

such familiar objects are quite predictable. In fact filmmakers often stage gigantic catastrophes (especially storms, crashes, and earthquakes) in miniature. They know that as long as the size *relationships* are realistic, you will not be conscious of the miniaturization.

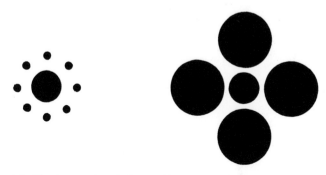

4-1. The two center circles are identical in size.

4-2. The three silhouettes of the man are identical in size.

We hardly ever encounter problems gauging the actual size of objects, because our experience is so reliable. In fact, our size/distance scaling is so dependable that most adults can easily and correctly match cards in their hands with cards on a table across a room, even though one image may be thirty-six times as wide as another! Even children as young as six years of age can accurately estimate the sizes of familiar objects in their natural surroundings. Without context clues, however, children perceived objects as smaller than actual size: in the absence of context they apparently responded more to the size of the retinal image. Many laboratory experiments designed to fool the eye depend for their effect on the elimination of context clues.

When the general context of an object is eliminated, you can become confused about its actual size. *Joe Sofa* is a case in point (Figure 4-3). The baseball glove is actually a leather-covered couch. Even with this knowledge it is difficult to imagine just how a person would fit in it. Simply including a doorway, lamp, or other familiar objects would have set us more at ease.

Perception of scale and measurement can be of critical importance to scientists. For this reason scientific photographs of unfamiliar objects often include a ruler or some familiar object such as a coin to orient the reader to the actual size.

SIZE SCALING IN ART

Unfortunately, books on art often fail to show the relative size of an artwork, even though it can be crucial to your concept of it. When you are told that Michelangelo's *David* is seventeen feet tall, you know vaguely that the statue is approximately as high as a two-story house, but to synthesize that knowledge with a photograph of the statue is not very satisfying. You can imagine the monumentality of this work much more clearly when you actually observe people dwarfed by the hugeness of the statue (Figure 4-4).

4-4. Michelangelo Buonarroti. *Moses.* Plaster cast from the original marble, 100 inches high, 1513–1515.(Permission Slater Memorial Museum, Norwich, Connecticut.) Cover up the woman in the picture to see how her presence affects your perception of the size of the sculpture.

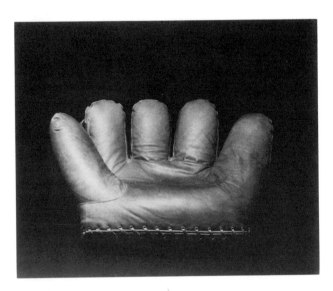

4-3. Paolo Lomazzi, Donato D'Urbino, and Jonathan De Pas. *Joe Sofa.* Polyurethane covered in leather, 33⅞ by 65¾ by 41⅜ inches, 1970. (Collection The Museum of Modern Art, New York. Gift of the manufacturer, Poltronova.)

Eliminating context within paintings causes interesting effects. By focusing on a fragment from a total situation, singling out objects almost never seen in isolation, and omitting the usual peripheral surroundings, the artist removes clues that ordinarily would orient you to object size. Pop artists in particular (notably James Rosenquist, Roy Lichtenstein, and Andy Warhol) have used such effects to lend a kind of ironic monumentality to common, ordinary objects. Surrounding an object by a lot of space yields the opposite effect, making it appear small (Figure 4-5).

Another way that artists make use of constancy scaling is by giving you a context guaranteed to confuse. The surrealist painter René Magritte often portrays familiar objects in combinations that conflict with your experience (Figure 4-6). Such images manipulate you in much the same way as the classic unanswerable question, "If the tree falls..." Because "The solution of mystery remains one of the most irresistible of all human temptations,"[1] many people engage in fruitless arguments about the "real" image: is it a normal rose in a dollhouse or a giant rose in a normal room? But such an image is purposeful: only by accepting the conflict and ambiguity can you begin to contemplate the artist's "real" intention.

4-5. (Copyright Volkswagen of America, Inc.)

4-6. René Magritte. *The Tomb of the Wrestlers.* Oil, 35 by 46 inches, 1960. (Permission Henry Torczyner, New York.)

A familiar use of size scaling by artists is the Renaissance method of perspective drawing, a mathematical system for determining how to portray the size of objects in a drawing or painting (Figure 4-7). This vanishing-point formula attempts to reproduce the image patterns of the retina, and objects at varying distances are depicted much as a camera would record the scene. Because this procedure seems to be scientific and objective, we have been taught to think that this type of perspective is essential for realistic appearances in artworks (see Chapter 6).

If we use the vanishing-point system as a "correct" standard, we find that beginning artists char-

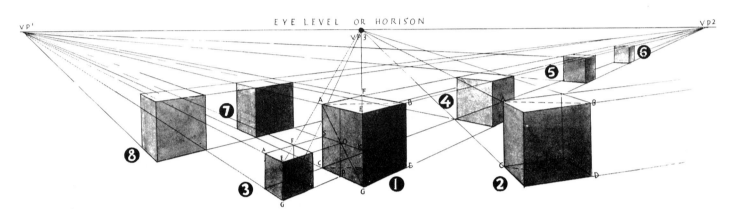

4-7. Relationships of cubes to the horizon line and vanishing points in linear perspective. (Reprinted from *How to Use Creative Perspective* by Ernest W. Watson, Van Nostrand Reinhold Company, 1955.)

4-8. Unkoku Togan. *Chinese Landscape.* (Permission Museum of Fine Arts, Boston. Weld Fenollosa Collection.)

acteristically draw objects too large in relation to one another. This is an effect of size constancy—that is, it represents a response to normal perception of object size rather than to the diminished size of the retinal pattern. For students learning traditional, realistic drawing and painting techniques, a working knowledge of vanishing points helps to counteract the influence of size constancy. The classic gesture of the artist—pencil at arm's length, one eye closed—is another aid to measuring relative image size in the scene being studied. Studies show that artists exhibit less size constancy than other people; this demonstrates an ability to break away from ordinary habits of seeing.

Children's art often shows a high degree of size constancy. Children do not generally change an object's size in a drawing to show distance. This is not because children cannot perceive size/distance relationships: in fact, in some circumstances children can judge distance and projected sizes even more accurately than adults. Children have not learned how to imitate the camera's viewpoint in their drawings. An extreme example of rigid size constancy is the child who was given a piece of clay and instructed to make an elephant. With shocked dismay she protested, "But there's not enough clay here to make an elephant!"

Oriental art has traditionally shunned the portrayal of outward appearance that is so much a part of our post-Renaissance western art. Oriental representation of size relationships differs from ours because it is not based on the retinal image. Figure 4-8 shows objects treated in harmony with size constancy. Three distances appear in the painting: near, far, and in between. All objects in the nearer distance—the buildings, the trees, the rocks—are painted a uniform size even though they are not meant to seem equidistant from the viewer. Objects at the far distance—the trees on and around the farthest mountains—are painted one uniform size, even though other clues in the picture show varying distances between them. The smaller, bent figure in the lower-left-hand corner is not a child: he is a servant, and his smaller size has nothing at all to do with retinal images—it is simply a matter of belittled status!

The custom of portraying the size of a person in relation to status can also be found in European medieval art, in which figures of Mary, Jesus, or saints are sometimes larger than the less divine persons around them. Medieval artists were aware of size/distance relationships, but size constancy exerted a stronger influence on their work than did the image sizes of the retina (Figure 4-9).

4-9. Pol de Limbourg. *Très Riches Heures du Duc de Berri,* February. C. 1415. (Permission Musée et Chateau de Chantilly.)

OTHER FACTORS AFFECTING SIZE PERCEPTION

In general, your visual perception is triggered by the retinal-image stimulus. In the case of size perception the mind reinterprets or corrects retinal information to conform to the constancy principle. You then perceive the mind's interpretation and not the direct sensory data from which it was formed. When any perception is removed in this way from direct sense information, it becomes increasingly vulnerable to modification by other factors.

One such influence is the emotional value of the stimulus. In a famous study children from poor homes and children from rich homes were shown coins and asked to estimate their size. A control group was asked to estimate the size of gray disks. The children who were shown the gray disks made the most accurate size estimates. All children who were shown the coins overestimated their size—the rich children to a slight extent and the poor children to a great extent. This finding is consistent with your own experience. If you are very hungry, a large serving of food may not look like enough (your eyes are bigger than your stomach!). Something unexpected or threatening may appear to be larger than it is (the wall suddenly loomed up in front of me!). And the fish that got away always seems to have been especially large!

Viewpoint is another mediating influence. Objects seen from below tend to be perceived as larger than they really are; objects seen from above seem smaller than they really are. This percept reflects experience: normally, you look up at something higher or larger than yourself, and you look down on things smaller or lower than yourself. Photographers and filmmakers take advantage of this phenomenon by placing cameras at high or low angles in order to distort apparent size.

Size constancy tends to break down over extreme distance. From an airplane or a skyscraper, objects no longer seem normal size: people appear to be ants; houses look like toys. Conscious reasoning plays a greater part in identifying the size of objects viewed from such distances.

FORM CONSTANCY

Look at Figure 4-10a. You can see a cube—not a flat pattern composed of the three shapes shown in Figure 4-10b. As a matter of fact, you will find it difficult to *see* Figure 4-10a as flat, even though it represents only three sides of the cube you imagine you see. Your mind completed or filled in unseen parts to fit your prepatterned idea of a total cube. Similarly, in Figure 4-11a your mind sees two squares overlapping, but your eyes are registering one square and one L-shape (Figure 4-11b). Again, you fill in an unseen portion in order to perceive a square. Here the principle of constancy applies to form or shape: the mind maintains an unchanging idea about the form of an object in spite of changes in the retinal-image shape caused by changing viewpoints. *Form constancy* is the specific way in which the mind applies two familiar strategies: filling in and correcting.

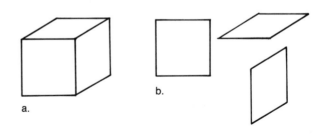

a.

b.

4-10.

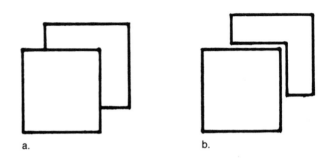

a.

b.

4-11.

To see *all* of a three-dimensional object at once is never possible. No matter where you look, some part is always hidden from view. You construct your idea of a whole object from your experiences with many objects seen from many viewpoints. Eventually, a partial view of an object will trigger perception of a whole object. Perception of the partial view then becomes equivalent to perception of the whole object, for your mind has filled in the missing data. At the same time your mind tunes out characteristics that are not relevant to the mental prepattern and in this way corrects the stimulus to fit a perceptual prejudice. Thus, again, you are gambling on probabilities. When you see a door, you expect it to open onto a closet, a room, or the outdoors. If you were to open a door and find a blank wall, you would be shocked. Similarly, when you look at Figure 4-12a, you do not suppose that its backside looks like Figure 4-12b, although after seeing it, you recognize the possibility.

Form constancy, then, is a means to make and operate on assumptions about the nature of whole objects in terms of the simplest and most probable forms. Tuning out all but the simplest probabilities is practical for everyday perception. The tendency to perceive wholes from parts, however, makes it possible for you to be manipulated by such things as films and advertisements. The movie set of the main street in a western town may be nothing more than a structure of flat storefronts. A fashion model's dress may actually be pinned and taped together in the back to give the illusion of stylish lines. In spite of the fact that we are continually exposed to such trickery and illusionism, we remain amazingly gullible!

DEPTH

You inhabit a three-dimensional universe. Most of your vision strategies are of a kind that supports survival in a world of space. This explains why many flat patterns are interpreted in terms of depth. A rectangular tabletop, for instance, registers in the retina as a trapezoid or parallelogram. Circular objects such as plates and glasses register as ellipses. As a result, when you see these flat patterns in certain contexts, they become illusions of shapes seen in the third dimension (Figure 4-13). Without the presence of the viewer's form constancy, artists could not represent space and depth on a flat surface. The shapes and patterns created by the artist trigger for the viewer a perception of wholes.

4-13.

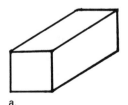

a.

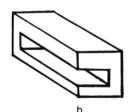

b.

4-12.

VISUAL LANGUAGE

An artist is involved in a communication process. He arranges stimuli that lead the viewer to complete in his own mind an image that the artist has only partially shown. An artwork, then, is a visual language by which certain signals transmit the meaning of a whole. If a viewer is to obtain closure or meaning, he must be able to "read" the language. Visual languages, like spoken languages, vary from culture to culture and from generation to generation. And—with typical pomposity—we classify our own language as somehow more "normal" and more "advanced" than anyone else's.

Our own tradition derives from the Italian Renaissance. It values the retinal image as the most "realistic" representation of an object and labels other types of pictorial language as unrealistic, primitive, or mad. We know through historical records, however, that other cultures consider their art to be highly realistic. Each culture develops conventions of visual language to represent those aspects of reality most valued by that particular culture.

Representing the external appearance of an object as seen from a single, fixed viewpoint in space (as the camera sees) requires distortion and correction of the actual nature of objects in the physical world. For example, the square sides of a cube must be distorted into trapezoids or parallelograms, and circular forms must be depicted as elliptical. Portions of objects must be omitted, for according to these rules you can only show what the eye can see. If it is taken to an extreme, this approach can result in strange images such as the one shown in Figure 4-14. We could defend this drawing as realistic according to our own rules. Even so, it looks like a weird two-legged creature! This example gives us an idea of the strangeness that other cultures might ascribe to our style of realism. Droodles (Chapter 1) draw our attention to the ridiculousness of literal interpretations of the retinal image. I wonder whether people of other cultures would find them humorous?

Some other methods of portraying objects permit different dimensions of form to be exposed and perceived. Isometric perspective, for example, has the advantage of providing more space in which to draw details, whereas vanishing-point perspective would diminish the same area (Figure 4-15). Isometric perspective is found in the art of medieval Europe, the Middle East, and the Orient, as well as in many other cultures.

4-14. Drawing copied from a Greek vase. (Permission Rudolph Arnheim, *Art and Visual Perception*, University of California Press, 1974.)

4-15. Ukiyo-e School. *Scenes of Kyoto: The Gion Festival and other Scenes* (detail from a six-panel folding screen). Japanese, seventeenth century. (Permission Museum of Fine Arts, Boston.)

Until children have been taught to perceive their drawings as inferior, they usually show little interest in drawing the distortions of the retinal image. Instead, they are strongly motivated to represent the most important charcteristics of the object in question. In doing this, children usually draw objects from the viewpoint that gives the most information. A wagon, for example, would be drawn from the side in order to show the wheels, tongue, and shape, whereas a house would be shown from the front. Ancient Egyptian art also does this (Figure 4-16). Images drawn on the tomb walls represented things that were to accompany the Pharaoh to his afterlife. Each image, therefore, had to include all the attributes considered characteristic. To ensure accuracy, such images—particularly of people—were drawn according to strict formulas.

The twentieth century has witnessed several movements in art that have broken away from the Renaissance commitment to the retinal image as the zenith of realistic representation. Paul Cézanne broke space and form into basic shapes without maintaining a fixed viewpoint. The cubists later carried this approach to an extreme by showing many views of an object simultaneously; ironically, this resulted in losing an immediate sense of the object, for cubist works require a great deal of

4-16. *The Sculptor Ipy and his wife receiving offering.* Tempera copy of Egyptian wall painting, New Kingdom, 1320–1200 B.C. (Permission The Metropolitan Museum of Art, New York.)

mental effort to assemble a perception of the image. Henri Matisse fought against the pretense of Renaissance picture-box illusionism and forthrightly portrayed the canvas as two-dimensional. He drew objects in a manner reflecting form constancy rather than retinal distortion. This upset viewers who were used to illusions of deep space, because the pictures seemed flat (Figure 4-17).

4-17. Henri Matisse. *The Red Studio*. Oil on canvas, 71¼ by 86¼ inches, 1911. (Collection The Museum of Modern Art. Mrs. Simon Guggenheim Fund.)

Many modern painters who have developed alternatives to Renaissance visual language have been accused of not showing things "as they are." But interestingly enough, Matisse's approach reflects a normal visual response that psychologists have termed *regression to the real object*. In perception experiments, subjects were shown certain shapes tilted in space and asked to draw the shape they saw, that is, the shape projected onto the retina. Subjects tended to interpret the retinal shape as closer to the real shape of the object than it actually was: for example, a plate seen sideways would be drawn rounder than the retinal image. These experiments show that even when you pay careful attention, your retinal patterns are perceived as resembling objects more than they actually do.

This is one reason why beginning or amateur painters often have a great deal of trouble with perspective. Their drawings tend to be influenced more by form constancy than by retinal image. Artists working with traditional realism must consciously train themselves to be sensitive to the retinal image.

ORIENTATION
Young children often look at books upside down without seeming to be aware that they are doing anything out of the ordinary. Indeed, researchers have found that children tend to ignore the spatial orientation of an object. Five-year-olds may not be able to distinguish between a shape and its mirror image even when the difference is pointed out to them. This is why some children have difficulty with letter reversals when they begin to read (especially with b, d, p, and q). After six years of age, children become increasingly sensitive to spatial orientation, although eleven-year-olds can still read a text turned at a ninety-degree angle more easily than adults can. Young children's drawings reflect this lack of concern with orientation: objects may float or be turned in many different directions within the space of the drawing. Children five to seven years of age show an awareness of spatial orientation when they put a line across the bottom of the drawing (*base line*) and relate everything in the picture to it.

In experiments with upside-down glasses, the retinal images are reversed in relation to normal vision. But after a short period of adjustment the subject perceives objects as right side up! It has also been found that concentrating on upside-down objects sometimes causes them to be seen right side up. Certain stimuli, however, become almost unrecognizable if they are turned upside down. For example, when faces are shown upside down in a movie, they do not "read" as upside-down faces but rather as monstrous faces whose foreheads contain mouths! Objects frequently seen from multiple viewpoints do not seem so subject to this effect. Just how and why we are affected by changes in the rotation of some objects but not others is not well understood. Most scientists seem to feel that more is involved than simple learning.

COLOR CONSTANCY
A blue wall looks blue in spite of a pattern of dappled sun and shadow. A lump of coal looks black and a piece of chalk looks white, regardless of whether they are seen in light or shadow. When you put on tinted sunglasses, you still see things as their normal color. Such experiences show you that some color constancy exists. The mind maintains a stable perception of the colors of objects in spite of changes in the retinal image. *Color constancy* has been more difficult to define, however, than the other constancies. Retinal response seems to provide less reliable sensory information about color than size or shape (Chapter 8). Your perception of color is influenced to such a great extent by memory and by context that in many cases you disregard retinal information. You take the "normal" color of objects so much for granted that you may be surprised to find that the rods (the photoreceptors used in night vision) do not register color. Unless some illumination stimulates the cones, night vision exists only in shades of gray.

When you try to perceive the color of some object for which you have no memory or association—say, a piece of paper of unknown color—your color perception results from the total pattern of brightness, illumination, and shadow. Experimental subjects viewing objects in a concealed context where shadows cannot be seen find color perception difficult and are often fooled. Color perception is mostly perception of relationships within a total context. While the actual color of an object may vary from situation to situation, its relationship to other objects within the context remains the same. This is why you can accommodate so quickly to pink light bulbs, tinted glasses, and slides shown on a colored wall. This is also why an artist's rendering of a scene can seem to have more fidelity than a color photograph. The artist is sensitive to the overall effect, whereas the camera mechanically records but does not make human judgments or adjustments.

Beginning painters often fail to realize the relative nature of color perception. Instead, they choose color on the basis of color constancy (green for grass, blue for water). The result may be unconvincing and discordant—even though each choice by itself is not wrong. Color is like an orchestra—each instrument may be playing the right melody, but unless all the instruments are tuned to some common tone, the result will be dissonance.

We should not be surprised to find that color constancy creates problems for art students. Color constancies in children are continually reinforced through coloring books, school ditto sheets, and adult reactions: Color the tree green. Color the sky blue. Make the car red. Oh, no! Leaves aren't purple! (see Figure 4-18). While such strategies do teach children the culturally agreed object color, they discourage sensitivity to the rich color effects in the environment and prevent the enjoyment of color as it registers on the retina. The impressionist painters in the late 1800s were very much aware of the ephemeral nature of color in the atmosphere, and they attempted to paint with an "innocent eye"—to look at colors, shadows, and reflections and to paint them as they appeared on the retina, not in terms of traditonal color constancies (see Figure C-7). This clear and conscious effort to become free of a perceptual prejudice has permitted viewers to enjoy the same experience—if only momentarily.

Practically speaking, constancy is an efficient strategy that keeps you from paying attention to objects and situations as if you were seeing them for the first time. It allows you to keep some stimuli in the background so that you can concentrate on others. By dealing automatically with recurring situations, constancies eliminate the need for constant evaluation and decision making and keep your perception orderly and stable. At the same time, however, they require you to tune out some of the variety inherent in perceptual experience, because constancies habituate you *not* to pay attention to some visual information. On the whole, constancy allows us to operate with security, with an optimistic confidence in the stability of things in a changing visual world.

4-18. "Educational" ditto sheet used in a Connecticut public school.

5. SPACE:

The Daily Odyssey

Have you ever walked along and—clunk!—stepped off a curb you hadn't been aware of? Or reached absent-mindedly to set down a glass on a table—only to find yourself sweeping up the pieces a few moments later? Such experiences are surprisingly rare, considering how automatic and unthinking your movements generally are. This is because most of your perceptual programming is made for a three-dimensional world. The senses of sight, hearing, and smell react to information coming to you from other points in space. Without a way of organizing this information you would live in a chaos of continually changing sensations. The retinal image would be "a world of pictures...which disappear and reappear capriciously."[1] The mind synthesizes and orders these perceptions with a survival program designed for a world of space.

The human perceptual system is so completely oriented to space that most people see Figure 5-1 as a circle on top of the paper rather than a ring. In an earlier discussion of figure and ground (Chapter 3) we found that one of the characteristics of a figure is that it seems to be *in front of* the ground; conversely, the ground is perceived as extending continuously *behind* the figure. In front of? Behind? Surely these are absurd terms for describing marks that are actually part of a flat, depthless surface! But they show that we are so oriented to space that we respond to flat stimuli with spatial perceptions.

Infant studies suggest that space perception is native to human development. As early as six months after birth a baby can tell the difference between a nearby rattle and a rattle three times larger at three times the distance, even though the retinal images are the same size. The Swiss psychologist Jean Piaget has observed and described a systematic—and seemingly universal—sequence of behavior showing that coherent perception of of space is constructed in infancy, step-by-painstaking-step.

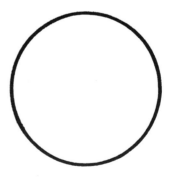

5-1.

THE BODY

We experience space with the motion of our bodies. We react—often violently—to interference with our freedom to move. Infants often rage at being penned in or pinned down. So do adults: people don't volunteer for prisons and straitjackets. We feel alive when we can move; we rejoice in space.

PERSONAL SPACE

Interestingly enough, each of us has a personal space "bubble," which we protect as an invisible, movable territory. We are not usually aware of it until we feel that someone else has intruded into it. Notice that when you talk to someone, you maintain a "natural" distance from each other, usually a distance comfortable for both of you. Occasionally, you encounter someone whose area of personal space is different from your own, and you feel uneasy: the other person is *keeping his distance*, *too close for comfort*, or *bearing down on you*. Try moving into another person's space bubble and see how he reacts—but be cautious!

Different cultures have different norms for personal space. Some ethnic groups establish wide spaces among people and talk with expansive gestures that define and maintain the space. Other groups value physical proximity and place themselves close enough to touch or even to breathe on one another while talking. Denial of a comfortable amount of personal space leads to frustration, hostility, and aggression. Animal experiments have produced fighters, killers, and cannibals by interfering with a species' normal space requirements. Humans appear to respond similarly. In military basic training aggressive violation of trainees' personal space is used as a tool for developing obedience through fear and frustration. Sociological research demonstrates that hostility and aggression emerge when living conditions do not meet personal and ethnic space requirements. Responsible architects, urban planners, and interior designers must take careful account of the human feelings that will result from their engineering of space.

The way your surrounding space is structured—the way you can or cannot move within it in relation to your immediate needs—largely determines how you will experience it. For this reason small rooms can seem either cosy and comforting or crowded and closed-in. Large rooms can seem either spacious and expansive or empty and anonymous. A well-designed space is flexible enough to accommodate the sometimes changing needs of the people who use it. Simply rearranging furniture in a room will change your relation to its space. Notice the furniture arrangements in homes you visit. The placement and movability of furniture express a family's sense of interpersonal space and distance.

The philosophy of an entire society is expressed through its architectural treatment of space. For example, in a medieval cathedral you feel awed and humble within the lacy, complex, upward-reaching spaces. Modern glass-and-steel buildings emphasize simplicity, efficiency, and technological power. Each time and culture reveals as well as imposes philosophical concepts of humankind by the way it structures public and private space (Figure 5-2).

5-2. Parish Hill High School, Chaplin, Connecticut. This school building was designed to promote a democratic philosophy of education. An authoritarian principal cannot stand in any one location and monitor the entire length of the circular corridor. (Designed by Joseph Salerno and Associates. Photograph by Bruce Thompson.)

THE OBSERVER

Your most powerful frame of reference is yourself. All your perceptions take place in the context of your own location in space. Besides vision other senses tell you of your location. Kinesthetic messages from your muscles tell you whether or not you are moving. The inner ear relays changes in motion and position to your brain. Hearing relates you to sound sources in the environment. Your skin sensations register temperature and air motion. Smells help you identify events and objects in your space environment. And the visual field itself—the origin of all your visual perception—belongs at any given instant *only* to you, the single person occupying that point in space and time. All perceptual information is received within the frame of reference of a person. Before spatial learning can take place, therefore, an infant must learn to perceive himself as an object located in space. His learning to locate other objects in space involves imagining the movements he would need to make in order to reach them. The mind organizes such experience into mental images or maps: some are highly conventionalized and shared by many people (road maps, repair manuals, seating charts); others are peculiarly individual.

Sometimes you are asked to discount your own location as a frame of reference. For example, in movie theaters the surroundings are darkened to eliminate peripheral clues that remind you of where you are. You can then project yourself into the motion picture, mentally detached from your physical location in space.

THE INNER EAR

The experience of space derives from other senses as well. Phylogenetic programming for space permeates your entire physiology. Hearing is a spatial sense. Your ears not only pick up sound but also inform you of its direction and source. Having two ears (*binaural hearing*) creates spatial coordinates because of the time and intensity differences between sounds received in each ear. Sensitivity to sound location can be learned and highly developed, especially by blind people and others whose survival depends on sound detection. Similarly, smell is a spatial sense. We can localize sources of odor because of the time and concentration differences between one nostril and the other.

One of the most highly developed anatomical structures is the *nonauditory labyrinth* in the inner ear—a tiny, complex structure where signals about body orientation and balance originate. You do not experience this area directly, because it is not connected to the higher centers of the brain. However, the labyrinth transmits signals through lower brain levels that cause reflex posture adjustments for maintaining body equilibrium.

Within the labyrinth of each ear are three *semicircular canals.* The canals are filled with a watery fluid that reacts to motion—somewhat like a jar of water. If you speed up, slow down, or change the direction the jar is moving in, the water will slosh against the sides of the jar until it reestablishes inertia. If the motion remains constant, the water eventually moves with it, and the sloshing ceases. You can swing a bucket of water around upside down without spilling it if you maintain constant speed, but when you stop, watch out! Much the same thing happens with the liquid in the semicircular canals. You may recall your childhood experiments with twirling around and around, then stopping—your surroundings seemed to keep on moving. This experience of dizziness and disequilibrium is caused by the continued motion of the fluid in the semicircular canals, which gradually subsides until inertia is recovered. You experience a similar adjustment period after a boat trip or carnival ride. When you are affected to the point of nausea, it is called *motion sickness.* Some people—dancers, sailors, aircraft pilots, and astronauts—learn to change their reactions to certain forces of rotation and gravity. Their adaptation apparently involves substituting visual, tactual, and kinesthetic signals that can override signals from the labyrinth.

Apparently, some people naturally put more trust in the visual field, letting it override information from the inner ear. Herman Witkin, a well-known psychologist, devised an experimental situation in which subjects sitting in a tilting chair were asked to orient themselves vertically to the earth. To confuse the situation, the subjects were placed in a small room that could itself be tilted by the experimenters. Some subjects tended to line themselves up with the room, while others disregarded what they saw and oriented themselves according to bodily sensations. Witkin called these styles *field dependent* and *field independent*, respectively. He found that these perceptual styles were consistent for an individual during a number of different experiments and that they correlated with some personality traits such as passivity or activity, dependence or independence, and shyness or self-confidence, respectively.

THE EYES

The structure of the eyes, apart from the retinal image, provides subtle clues for judging distance, but they are generally of little real significance.

The nearer an object is, the more the eyes must turn inward toward each other in order to focus the image on each fovea: this turning is called *convergence*. Convergence is geater for close objects than for distant ones (Figure 5-3). You can easily observe convergence in another person: ask him to hold his index finger at arm's length and to slowly bring the finger toward his face while focusing on it. As his finger comes closer, his eyes will turn in towards each other until he eventually appears cross-eyed.

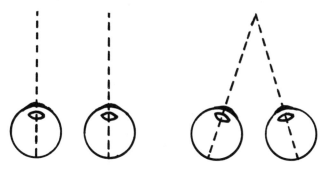

5-3. Convergence.

Convergence produces tensions in the muscles holding and turning the eyeballs (Chapter 2). This tension is signaled to the brain, giving some information about the distance of the object. Convergence is a weak cue for distance perception, but more significant for close than for distant objects.

Another muscular movement occurs in the ciliary muscle surrounding the crystalline lens: it expands or contracts the lens to direct the focal point precisely onto the retina. In theory, these movements, called *accommodation*, could provide subtle depth cues, but experiments reveal that even at short distances they are such a weak factor that they can hardly be effectively isolated for experimentation.

Each eye sees a slightly different image (Chapter 2). This phenomenon is known as *binocular disparity*. Hold a finger (or anything else) several inches from your face; look at it first with one eye and then with the other. You will notice that one eye sees more of one side and the other eye sees more of the other side. With two eyes, then, you are actually seeing a little way *around* an object—something that would be impossible with a single eye, except by moving the head (which is how people compensate when they are blind in one eye). With a little experimentation you will find that the difference between these two images is much greater for close objects than for distant ones. In fact, for distances greater than twenty feet, the disparity is too little to be effective. Disparity is a significant factor in depth perception only for relatively near objects.

Binocular disparity has been used as the basis for constructing illusions of depth in two dimensions. The principle is simple: if you place two cameras two and one-half inches apart (approximately the distance between the eyes) and take two pictures, you will have a picture of what each eye sees. If you then present each picture separately to each eye, the viewer will experience realistic, three-dimensional effects. It works: remember the Viewmaster? If you were lucky, you may have seen an old Victorian stereopticon, a popular entertainment in the nineteenth century (Figure 5-4). Today, you can sometimes find them in antique shops. Over the past century many different stereoscopic devices have been designed; some work better than others.

In the mid-fifties, 3-D motion pictures were produced. Separate images were projected simultaneously onto the screen by light polarized in two different planes. The viewer was required to wear cardboard glasses in which each lens was made of film polarized to admit only one image, thereby maintaining separate right- and left-eye inputs to the brain (Figure 5-5). These movies remained only a novelty, probably because of competition from Cinerama, which also produced breathtaking depth effects but without the nuisance of glasses.

Stereoscopy is not only entertaining. Very practical applications have been made of the fact that disparity is a deterrent to image fusion. Fusion will occur only when the images are sufficiently similar. When images are too dissimilar, fusion does not take place: instead, retinal rivalry occurs (Chapter 2). Because we are extremely sensitive to even a slight disparity, the stereoscope is a good device for detecting small differences between similar images. Stereoscopic viewing of a counterfeit bill and a genuine one will clearly expose minute differences. Microphotos of different bullets viewed stereoscopically can reveal whether or not they have been fired from the same gun. Stereoscopic aerial photos reveal areas of camouflage that would not show in a single photograph. Stereoscopic cards are used with certain vision-testing and training instruments.

THE VISUAL FIELD

Normal, everyday perception of space and depth is organized from the interaction of many aspects of the visual field. Even when these factors are not individually reliable, they provide cross-checks for one another. Depth perception is rather like a house of cards: the total structure is interdependent, and withdrawing key supports can cause the whole structure to collapse. As we consider perceptual factors separately, you must bear in mind that—apart from artificial situations in the laboratory or in art—perception rarely depends on a single factor.

5-5. Viewers watch a 3-D movie. (J. R. Eyerman, Time-Life Picture Agency © Time, Inc.)

5-4. This reconstruction of a Brewster lenticular-prism stereoscope was manufactured for vision training. (Photograph by Bruce Thompson.)

GENERAL RELATIVITY

You perceive space and distance best when the visual field consists of familiar objects in familiar contexts. It is difficult or impossible to accurately estimate the size or distance of objects when you cannot relate them to something else in the visual field. For this reason, researchers can easily fool experimental subjects by isolating stimuli.

Traditionally, artists have relied on the principle of relativity to represent familiar objects in familiar relationships. The viewer brings to bear his past experience and for the most part sees what he expects to see. Traditional artworks support rather than challenge a viewer's normal perceptual processes. Paintings that show familiar objects in familiar relationships, such as landscapes and still lifes, have always remained popular in spite of many profound movements and experiments in art. A simple and direct use of relativity is shown in Figure 5-6. Cover and uncover the distant ship on the right of the composition; notice how its presence enhances your sense of space.

5-6. Winslow Homer. *Breezing Up.* Oil on canvas, 24⅛ by 38⅛ inches, 1876. (Permission National Gallery of Art, Washington, D.C., Gift of the W. L. and May T. Mellon Foundation.)

Now look at Figure 5-7. How difficult it is to find a consistent sense of space! Familiar and unfamiliar objects are juxtaposed in ways that are quite alien to everyday notions of how things are located in space. You can find spatial qualities in small areas of the painting, but the artist effectively and purposefully prevents you from applying everyday perceptual techniques to the painting as a whole. This painting presents a highly personal, mental map of ships; it denies objective space and affirms subjective, nonrational sensibilities. It shows not outward but inward space.

CONSTANCY

Constancies of size, form, and color are the source of a powerful visual language. An artist has a tremendous amount going for him at the outset, since the viewer will bring to the artwork all his perceptual constancies and prejudices. In many examples throughout this book you have seen how powerfully these prejudices operate. As long as an artist portrays objects and relationships for which you have norms, you can read size, space, and depth with security. But when an artist employs objects, relationships, or distances with which you have had no past experience, it is difficult or impossible to feel comfortable judging size or distance in the usual way. Artists can challenge your customary perceptions and prod you to experience alternatives.

In Figure 5-8 you can read distance between objects, because they are assumed to be approximately equal in size and their images become smaller and less sharp as you look upward from the bottom of the picture—yet it is difficult to feel oriented to the whole scene. Any assumption about the "real" size of the objects is impossible. Are they miniature? Microscopic? Gigantic? Are they the size of chairs and couches—as a literal interpretation of the title would suggest—or is the title symbolic? Because you lack past experience with these objects, the painting represents a world apart from physical reality, a universe that operates according to its own laws, a metaphysical vision of time.

5-7. Marc Chagall. *I and the Village.* Oil, 75⅝ by 59⅝ inches, 1911. (Collection The Museum of Modern Art, New York. Mrs. Simon Guggenheim Fund.)

5-8. Yves Tanguy. *The Furniture of Time.* Oil on canvas, 45¾ by 35 inches, 1939 (Collection of James Thrall Soby.)

FIELD AND FRAME

Both photographs in Figure 5-9 show the same tree, yet one seems much closer to you than the other. This powerful orientation to space and distance comes from the relationship of the subject to the borders of the composition. A wide-angle, panoramic scene gives you a sense of viewing from a distance and a strong feeling of removal from the subject (Figure 5-10). A restricted view, on the other hand, gives you a feeling of proximity to the subject. This pictorial definition of the field of vision is called the *field-and-frame relationship*. The field is what is in the composition, and the frame is its perimeter. The field-and-frame relationship is effective because it parallels normal visual experience: from a distance many things register on your retinal field; conversely, when you confront a large object or peer closely at an object, it fills your visual field, and you don't see the surrounding context.

Movie directors use the field-and-frame relationship to control the emotional involvement of the audience. *Long shots* are used for objective, complete, often impersonal representations; *closeups* are used to generate a personal, gut-level involvement in scenes of love, violence, or other intense emotion. Frequent movie and television viewing—in which field and frame are so easily controlled—have habituated us so completely to prepro-grammed involvement that many people feel a frustrating sense of distance from live theater performances, where emotional involvement and focus are much more a consequence of the viewer's own selection processes.

VERTICAL POSITIONING

You raise your eyes to see distant things and lower your eyes to look at objects nearer to you: most of your visual experience follows this pattern. Artists reflect this when they place nearer objects toward the bottom of a picture and more distant ones higher up. The objects usually relate to a horizon line at an imaginary eye level so that the eye moves upward to reach the horizon and downward to look at the "nearer" objects. Objects that do not relate to a horizon line may appear to be floating (Figures 5-7 and 5-14). Position in the picture plane is a reliable and universally used indicator of relative distance (Figures 4-8, 4-9, 4-15, 4-17, 5-6, 5-8, and 6-4). There are some exceptions, notably in the positioning of objects above the horizon such as clouds or ceilings: as their distance increases, they descend from the top of the picture downward toward the horizon (Figure 5-10). Aerial views are another exception: object positions radiate outward as they increase in distance from a focal point (Figure 5-2).

5-9. (Reprinted from *Graphic Perception of Space* by Frank Mulvey, Van Nostrand Reinhold Company, 1969.)

5-10. El Greco. *View of Toledo*. Oil on canvas, 47¾ by 42¾ inches, 1541–1614. (Permission The Metropolitan Museum of Art. Bequest of Mrs. H. O. Havemeyer, 1929. The H. O. Havemeyer collection.) This panoramic scene removes the viewer to a god-like position, an omnipotent overview. Objects within the composition approach the horizon as they increase in distance from the imaginary viewpoint.

INTERPOSITION

As you saw in Chapter 4, your tendency to complete and categorize forms causes Figure 5-11a to read as two overlapping squares rather than two contiguous jigsaw-puzzle shapes (5-11b) or an oddity such as 5-11c. To further cloud the issue, seeing this figure as overlapping squares adds to constancy and completion the additional factor of space—for overlapping involves spatial relationships such as *on top of*, *in front of*, *in between*, and *behind*. How can it be simpler to see two squares (that aren't there) in a three-dimensional relationship (that isn't there either)—rather than in the simple, flat pattern that actually *is* there? Apparently our programming for a spatial world so dominates our perception that we are compelled to interpret flat stimuli in terms of space!

Overlapping is technically called *interposition*, which means that an object is positioned in between the viewer and another object. In Figure 5-11 you perceive the left-hand square as if it were placed between yourself and the "square" on the right. The experience of interposition is basic to everyday vision, since it is impossible to see any three-dimensional object in its entirety at once: some part of the object is always masked—either by other objects or by intervening surfaces of the object itself (except for fully transparent objects). Some researchers feel that the perception of interposition is the strongest cue for perceiving depth.

When interposition is perceived, a more completely seen figure is perceived as being in front of another, less completely seen figure. In Figure 5-12a the three circles appear to be equally distant from you: they are all complete. In Figure 5-12b, however, the center circle alone maintains completeness and therefore is automatically read as being on top of the others. What can be defined as a complete figure lies within a precariously limited range of normal shapes, as you can see from the third grouping (Figure 5-12c). With the irregular shapes it is impossible to tell which one is supposed to be on top. With a little concentration you can perceive a number of different overlap combinations.

Artworks that represent *any* degree of interposition will always appear to have more depth than compositions that do not. The drawings of children and untrained artists often lack overlapping and seem "flat." Painters and photographers use interposition to great advantage when they employ such devices as overhanging branches or foreground areas of rocks, bushes, or blades of grass that overlap a more distant scene (Figure 5-13). The complex overlapping of parts of the body (*foreshortening*) is a major reason for the quality of depth characteristic of the drawings and frescoes of Michelangelo (Figure 5-14). Because he was a sculptor, Michelangelo's two-dimensional works reflect a special awareness of space.

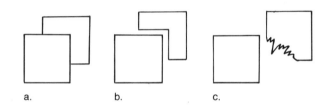

a.   b.   c.

5-11.

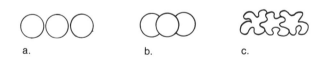

a.   b.   c.

5-12.

5-13. Thomas Cole. *The Pic-Nic.* Oil on canvas, 47 by 71¾
inches, 1846. (Permission The Brooklyn Museum, A. Augustus
Healy Fund.) Skillful combinations of depth cues give an illusion
of space in this painting. The field-and-frame relationship
promotes a sense of distance both from and within the scene.
The landscape ascends toward the horizon with distance; the
clouds descend. Among the trees, people, and hills each and
every interposition is a depth indicator, creating a network of
perceptual closures.

5-14. Michelangelo Buonarroti. *The Deluge* (detail from the
ceiling of the Sistine Chapel). Fresco, 1508–1512. (Permission
The Vatican, Rome.)

With transparent objects you see overlapping and the total form at the same time. Consequently, drawings that show overlapping and complete form simultaneously represent the experience of transparency and produce a perception of depth (Figure 5-15). Very often drawings of this type are ambiguous, since, although you recognize the overlapping, you have no way of telling which surface is supposed to be on top. Because they can be perceived in alternate ways, such drawings are often called *reversible illusions*. Perhaps transparent glass and plastic objects are universally fascinating and valued because their very nature presents us with a similar visual paradox.

5-15.

MOTION PARALLAX

Interpositions are subject to continual change. You have only to shift the position of your head slightly to alter the relationships among objects to your visual field. Change in the relationships of objects to one another in the retinal image due to motion of the head or body is called *motion parallax*. You can become very aware of motion parallax when you ride in a car or train. As you travel through wooded areas, motion parallax among trees is a dizzy, flickering experience: the world seems to be whirling by. When you move through open, spacious landscapes, you can imagine that you are traveling on the outermost rim of a gigantic disk: near objects fly by so rapidly that they register as blurs, while more distant objects "move" less. Objects in outer space are *so* far away that *no* distance or speed you travel is sufficient to produce motion

parallax. Hence, objects such as the moon do not seem to change position in spite of parallax effects in the landscape. Because the moon seems to keep a constant distance, it appears to follow you.

Our visual experience of movement in space is produced by a continuous succession of changing images. Even slight head motion enhances the experience of space. But when you stand in front of a painting and move your head, the objects represented in the composition do not change in relation to one another. Lack of motion parallax tells you that you are looking at a flat surface. Science may provide future artists with a tool for overcoming this basic limitation. Holographic photography produces uncanny two-dimensional photographs in which motion parallax *can* be experienced. A *hologram* is a recorded pattern of interference between reflected and projected portions of a split laser beam. Looking at a holographic plate is rather like looking into a box or a diorama and being able to move your head around to inspect the objects—only the box doesn't exist—you are looking at what appears to be a flat, plastic film! (A full explanation of holograms is beyond the scope of this book, but readers interested in this fascinating subject will find some references in the Bibliography.)

Movie directors must be concerned with motion parallax. A flat backdrop behind the actors does not give a realistic illusion of depth, even when it moves, because the motion parallax is missing.

Motion parallax is an important aspect of looking at sculpture. Because the sculptor deals with forms in space, he is deeply involved in the changing relationships among parts of the sculpture as they are seen from various locations. Unlike the painter, whose work can be seen only from a frontal view, the sculptor must create an image that is satisfying from many viewpoints (Figure 7-11).

CONCEPTUAL AND VISUAL SPACE

We have often referred to preexisting mental norms and constancies that dictate how you will perceive visual images. The process of perception seems endlessly involved in correcting disparities between what we *do* see and what we *want* to see. An object that does not conform to a standard category is a stumbling block to closure. One way in which your mind can accept the "imperfect" stimulus is to account for it as a variation or deviant form of a standard classification. This is rather like explaining lizards by saying that they are merely snakes with legs—a neat solution that keeps you from having to look at lizards as things in their own right. Similarly, with vision your mind will look for a simple solution to get you off the hook and allow you to avoid dealing with peculiarities in the stimulus. Because you have a vast network of mental categories that function for objects in space, you may expect to find that many flat images are perceived as variations or distortions of three-dimensional space.

The square (Figure 5-16a) is easily seen as a flat, undistorted figure: it fits two standard categories—your concept of a square and the retinal image of a square seen straight on. Figure 5-16b is slightly more complicated but still simple enough to fit the conceptual category of a flat shape (a rhombus) or the visual-image category of a square tilted in space. When only four lines are added to the rhombus, however, the conceptual circuit is overloaded: the image no longer fits any standardized group of flat figures, and you opt for a visual-image category of the space world and see a table (Figure 5-16c). The same is true for the cube (Figure 5-16d): the perception of least resistance occurs in the visual category of a solid cube in space as it is registered on the retina.

Experiments show, however, that this type of pictorial depth perception is extensively conditioned by culture. African tribal subjects whose art did not include representation of visual space did not perceive depth in pictures that used western pictorial depth cues. Also, because they did not perceive drawings according to retinal-image categories, they saw no ambiguity in a drawing similar to Figure 5-17 and were able to draw it from memory more easily than westernized subjects.

People may have difficulty comprehending that something as basic as vision is culturally based. School personnel sometimes test "depth" perception by showing pupils flat patterns that represent drawings of three-dimensional solids. Children who make errors are said to lack depth perception and may be labeled as perceptually handicapped. It is important to realize that such tests do not test actual depth perception but merely whether or not the child is sufficiently acculturated to read flat patterns in the culturally desired way.

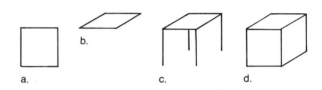

5-16.

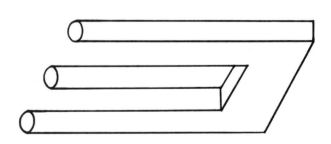

5-17. Ambiguous trident, an irresolvable image.

The isometric cube (Figure 5-18a) apparently offers a fine compromise between conceptual and visual norms in representing space two-dimensionally. It is universally acquired by children, who find it satisfying and continue to use it, unless they are retrained by adults. It has been used throughout the world in many time periods and in both "primitive" and "advanced" cultures, yet it is quite different from the retinal or camera image of a cube (Figure 5-18b). Is there something "natural" about the isometric cube that causes it to be preferred so often?

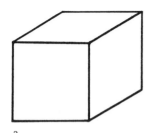 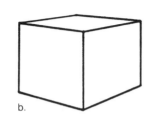

a.

b.

5-18. (a.) Isometric or conceptual cube. (b.) Vanishing-point perspective or visual cube.

The isometric cube expresses some characteristics of our conceptual idea of a cube: the front plane is symmetrical and undistorted, and it preserves the equal sides and right angles of a real cube; its side and top are represented by parallelograms that sacrifice right angles but maintain all the integrity of parallel and equal sides. Ironically, the visual cube—which fits our idea of "realistic" representation better—shows less correspondence with the *concept* of a cube: all sides are transformed into trapezoids and quadrangles, destroying more than half of the parallel relationships and all of the right angles that exist in a real cube. You might well wonder why the visual cube has come to be accepted as a more realistic representation.

The answer seems to lie in the fact that the art of any culture represents those aspects of reality that are held in highest esteem by that culture. With the exception of post-Renaissance western art, the precise location of the viewer in space has not been isolated as an important determinant of how space should be represented. Other times and other cultures have focused on other dimensions of reality. The ancient Egyptians, for example, considered it important to include every meaningful detail about a subject. In medieval art metaphysical expressions dominate. Hunting tribes often include the internal organs of animals in their drawings, showing a kind of X-ray awareness. Oriental art frequently prefers an imagined viewpoint well above the earth. The realities expressed through art are as rich and various as the dimensions of human experience. All people's preferences in art are biased in favor of their own cultural values: we are not different. The next chapter describes some of the historical developments that led to our commitment to the retinal image.

6. DEPTH AND DISTANCE:

The "I" as a Camera

Look around the room and notice how the appearance of things changes when they are further away from you. Parallel lines in the floor or ceiling seem to come closer together. Horizontal edges appear to slant. Textures seem to compress. Details are harder to see. These gradual changes in the appearance of objects because of their increasing distance from you are called *perceptual* or *distance gradients*.

Gradients constitute a different class of distance cues from those described in the last chapter. Interposition, position, and motion parallax give you information that can be directly verified: that is, you can walk around in space, examine the objects, and figure out whether your eyes are giving you correct information.

Gradients, however, do not exist in space. They disappear as you approach objects. Railroad tracks appear to converge at a point on the horizon, but if you walk to that point, you will find them to be the same distance apart as they were where you started. The convergence does not exist. Similarly, distant houses are not really smaller than houses close by. Far objects do not have less detail than near objects. Although these gradients register on the retina, they are not characteristic of objects in the physical world.

Gradients belong to the *visual field*—the image of the external world that registers on the retina at a given point in time and space. The visual field differs from the physical world in several important ways. The physical world surrounds you on all sides—three hundred sixty degrees—but your visual field at any given instant is generally shaped like an oval that extends approximately one hundred eighty degrees horizontally and one hundred fifty degrees vertically (Figure 6-1). The physical world has no central focus, but your visual field is sharp and clear at the center and increasingly vague toward the periphery. Gradient patterns that register on the retina depend on the viewer's position in space, and they change with every change in the viewer's location.

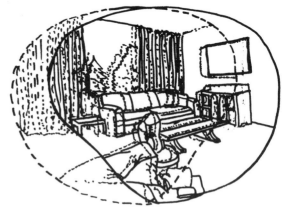

6-1. The visual fields and images seen in the right and left eyes are shown by solid and dotted lines, respectively. (Composite drawing adapted from Mach, Bower, and Gibson.)

PATTERN DENSITY

The distance effects the Figure 6-2 are produced by gradients of *density* or *interval*. The dots or lines become gradually more densely concentrated, and the spaces between them become increasingly smaller. This pattern of general compression produces a perception of space and distance. When density gradients occur in a regular pattern (Figure 6-2a and b), the effect is of a single, continuous surface extending into space. When sudden or irregular changes occur in the rate of the gradient, you perceive a change in planes: in Figure 6-2c an invisible line seems to show something like a step where the gradient rate abruptly changes. The rate of change in a gradient tells you your relation in space to the surface. When you look straight-on at a surface (such as checkerboard), the pattern change is very much less than when you look at the surface from a slant.

Some researchers feel that density gradients may be the most effective depth cue. In a well-known series of experiments babies of a variety of species (including human) were placed on a sheet of heavy glass through which they could see checkerboard surfaces at varying depths below them. Because the glass offered solid support, the perception of a drop-off point was purely visual, and the arrangement was called a *visual cliff* (Figure 6-3). All species showed reluctance, refusal, and sometimes terror at the prospect of crossing over the "deep" side, even though they could touch and feel the glass that made it perfectly safe to do so. The experiments indicated that babies of all species show visual depth perception as soon as they are able to move about—for some this is within hours of birth. Further, the visual cues of pattern density and motion parallax completely overwhelmed the effectiveness of other factors in the situation, including tactual evidence and reward incentives.

Some evidence shows that perception of the gradient—not perception of the surface per se—is what leads to the perception of depth. That is, any gradient pattern will give depth effects. For this reason geometric patterns, which can be mathematically controlled, show more dramatic illusions of depth than patterns representing natural scenes, which are variable and less rigidly patterned. Both

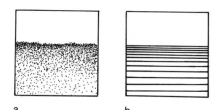

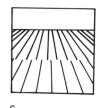

a.   b.   c.

6-2.

6-3. The visual cliff. (Permission *Scientific American, Inc.* and William Vandivert.) The kitten is standing on a sheet of heavy glass. You can see the kitten's-eye view if you close one eye and look at the picture from directly above the kitten's head.

optical and representational artists use pattern density to create illusions of depth in two dimensions (Figures 4-13, 5-8, 5-13, and 6-4).

6-4. Vincent van Gogh. *The Crau from Montmajour*. Pen and ink,
19 by 24 inches, 1888. (Permission British Museum, London.)

DETAIL

You are able to see less and less detail as things become further away. Within limits you may find that focusing on an object seems to bring it nearer. Focusing causes the image to fall on the fovea, where you have the greatest visual acuity; the increased perception of detail results in a sense of nearer distance.

Leonardo da Vinci termed the gradient of detail the *perspective of disappearance* and defined it as how objects in a picture "ought to be less finished in proportion as they are remote."[1] An ancient Chinese treatise states the same principle as, "Distant men have no eyes; distant trees have no branches."[2] Because greater detail is characteristic of nearer distance, an artist can make objects seem nearer by increasing the amount of detail, while a gradual phasing out of detail creates the illusion of distance. In Figure 6-5 *all* objects are weighed down with a wealth of detail. In real life you would have to be very close to the subject in order to see the amount of detail shown here—much closer than the field/frame orientation suggests—indeed, you would need to be within inches of it or peering through a magnifying glass! This painting symbolically violates your personal space by portraying detail characteristic only of intimate contact: the effect is psychologically oppressive and suffocating. In striking contrast is the naturalism of Jan Vermeer, a seventeenth-century Dutch artist (Figure 6-6). Vermeer places the sharpest detail in the area of the woman's hands and decreases the amount of detail outward from this point. Vermeer mirrors your normal visual field when he shows the greatest detail in an area of natural interest and focus. This is one reason why Vermeer paintings are comfortable and pleasant to look at.

With increasing distance the retinal image becomes less detailed and more general. Consequently, when you see things at a distance, less visual information is registered in the retina, and you must rely more on past experience. When the environment is familiar, you make few errors in identification, because you usually see what you expect to see. But in unfamiliar territory your experience may be different. In a strange neighborhood you have to come very close to a street sign in order to read it, even though in your own neighborhood you might recognize a familiar sign from a much greater distance. You can identify your best friend two blocks away, but if you're watching for someone whom you have seen only once or twice, he may have to come within ten feet before you are certain that he is the right person. And the time and error involved in trying to find unfamiliar signs and landmarks on a vacation trip often contributes to a general feeling of irritability. In a traditional painting such as *The Pic-Nic* (Figure 5-13) the artist needs to portray distant hills, trees, and mountains only in a general way: you can identify them instantly, and you are not confused when details are omitted. *The Furniture of Time* (Figure 5-8), however, is unfamiliar territory. As you scrutinize and puzzle over the strange forms, the disappearing detail is significant—it frustrates your search for meaning.

6-5. Ivan Albright. *Into The World There Came a Soul Called Ida.*
Oil, 55 by 46 inches, 1928–29. (Permission Ivan Albright and The
Art Institute of Chicago.)

6-6. Jan Vermeer. *The Lacemaker.* Oil, 9⅞ by 8¼ inches, 17th century. (Cliches des Musees Nationaux, Paris.)

SHARPNESS

As distance increases, the edges of objects seem less distinct, more blurred. Determining where one object ends and the next one begins becomes more difficult as things seem to merge into one another. With a highly textured surface such as a plowed field the texture becomes increasingly compressed until it gradually merges into a uniform surface (Figure 6-7). Because of this effect artists often suggest distance by portraying backgrounds in a blurred manner. This effect also occurs in photographs, for gradients register on the film in much the same way as they do on the human retina.

The block portrait in Figure 6-8 produces a dramatic result when the sharpness of the squares is lost due to distance. At reading distance the squares and their edges are quite distinct. If you view this mosaic from a distance of about twelve feet, however, you can readily identify the face of a well-known American. Squinting or rapidly moving the portrait may also prompt recognition, for both these techniques have the effect of blurring the edges of the squares. In this case by seeing less you are able to see more! The scientists who produced this and other block portraits were trying to find the minimum amount of information necessary for the recognition of faces. Amazingly enough, they found that they could get recognition levels up to ninety-five percent correctness when a face photograph was reduced to a composition of sixteen-by-sixteen squares using eight or sixteen shades of gray.

6-7. (Photograph by Bruce Thompson.)

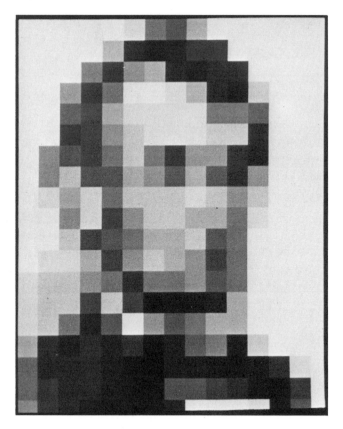

6-8. Block portrait. (Permission Leon D. Harmon and *Scientific American, Inc.*)

COLOR

Color gradients are especially noticeable in landscapes. As objects recede into the distance, their colors appear less intense, paler, more grayish or bluish. Color gradients usually show up only across great expanses of space. This effect is commonly represented in landscape paintings and registers automatically in color photographs. Over short distances color gradients are difficult to separate from the effects of light and shadow, because color perception is influenced so much by familiarity with the object (Chapter 8). Under artificial laboratory conditions some experiments show that bright objects are perceived as nearer to the observer than less bright objects, but researchers do not agree on the extent or significance of this as a distance cue. Regardless of what laboratory tests show, color gradients *do* evoke illusions of depth and distance, and they are used effectively by artists, as is clearly shown in Figures 6-9 and C-1. In both paintings all other depth cues—size, position, interposition, and definition of edges—remain constant; the pronounced depth effects result from color variation alone.

In the study of art three distance gradients—detail, sharpness, and color—are commonly grouped together and called *aerial perspective*, since they seem to be caused by the increasing volume of air through which objects are seen. Fog and the haze of air pollution cause the same effects over shorter distances. We exclaim ecstatically, "What a clear day!" when we see distant objects with unaccustomed brilliance and clarity. Leonardo da Vinci is often given credit for first describing aerial perspective and explaining its use in painting. During the Renaissance aerial perspective was a favored technique for representing space and distance.

6-9. Wu Chen. *Bamboo in the Wind.* 29⅝ by 21⅜ inches, 1280–1354. (Permission Museum of Fine Arts, Boston. Chinese and Japanese Special Fund.)

LIGHT AND SHADOW

You live in a world of light and shadow. Shadow helps you perceive the volume, solidity, texture, and form of objects. Indeed, with shadow alone you can "see" an invisible object—the shadow letters in Figure 6-10, for example. Similarly, you interpret high-contrast photographs by reading the shadows (Figures 3-13 and 3-14).

Without shadows the effect of an image is flat. This is the reason why snapshots taken with flash-bulbs often lack the apparent depth of photographs with softer, more pleasant shadow gradients from natural lighting. Because of our visual tradition artworks that do not use shading may strike you as flat—a quality often attributed to Japanese prints, Egyptian tomb paintings, medieval art, and works by modern artists who use uniform areas of color (Manet, Gauguin, Matisse, Miró, Modigliani, and others).

You can think of light as creating a spherical gradient of illumination. The pattern of shadow depends on the orientation of an object to the source of light: surfaces that face the light source are lighter, while opposing surfaces are in shadow. (We are speaking here of an *attached shadow*, which is part of the perceived surface of the object, as opposed to a *cast shadow*, which falls onto a surface outside the object.) The distribution and progression rate of brightness and darkness across a surface tell you the shape of the object. Gradual transitions from light to shadow yield the perception of a curved surface; sudden changes from light to dark read as a sharp corner or a change in planes (Figure 6-11). When you look at pictures, you automatically assume that the light source is above and to the left, unless you have reason to believe otherwise. Just how powerfully this assumption operates can be seen in Figure 6-12.

The manipulation of light-to-dark gradients is one of the first systems traditionally taught to drawing students. Dark, shaded areas appear to recede from the viewer, while light areas and highlights appear to project toward the viewer. The play of light and dark in the composition of an artwork is called *chiaroscuro* (from two Italian words meaning "light" and "dark"). Chiaroscuro was developed during the Renaissance as a way of creating a

6-10.

6-11. (Photograph by Bruce Thompson.)

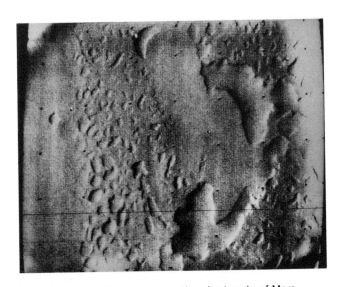

6-12. Pits and hollows in the south polar terrain of Mars. (Courtesy Jet Propulsion Laboratory, California Institute of Technology, Pasadena.) Turn this picture upside down to see the depressions become bumps.

88

powerful illusion of depth on a flat surface. Symbolic as well as visual aspects of light and darkness are especially characteristic of works by later artists such as Caravaggio, Rembrandt, and Goya (Figure 6-13).

Shadows are capricious. They change constantly— with time of day, wattage of light bulbs, placement of lamps, and changes in your own location. Although you depend on shadow for visual information about the form of an object, you are not usually aware of it as a quality separate from the object itself. You usually discount the shadow and exclude it from conscious perception of the object. After all, shadows change, but objects do not.

SIZE GRADIENTS

As an object increases in distance from you, its image on the retina becomes smaller (Chapter 4). You can think of this size/distance relationship as a gradient, because it involves an apparent gradual change in an attribute of the object as its distance from you increases. Throughout history, artists have differed widely in the extent to which they have represented this phenomenon. Little, if any, use of size gradients to represent distance is found in the art of ancient Egypt and Greece or the art of

6-13. Michelangelo Merisi da Caravaggio. *Supper at Emmaus.* Oil on canvas, 56 by 77½ inches, 1598–1600. (Permission National Gallery, London.)

"primitive" cultures, because for these groups the most valued aspects of reality are not involved with spatial relationships. Paintings by medieval artists (Figure 4-9) and "naive" artists such as Grandma Moses (Figure 6-14) often do show objects smaller as they become more distant, but even here the painting may not look quite "right"; we then announce that the artist did not use "perspective." What we really mean is that the artist did not use the system of perspective to which *we* are habituated: *vanishing-point perspective*, sometimes called *linear* or *Renaissance perspective*.

VANISHING-POINT PERSPECTIVE

In essence, vanishing-point perspective is a mathematically based system for representing the size gradients that occur in a single retina at a particular location in space. It is a camera's-eye view, but it antedated the camera by nearly four hundred years! The basis of vanishing-point perspective is most familiarly illustrated by railroad tracks. Seen from a given point in space, the parallel lines converge or vanish at some point on the horizon (Figure 6-15). Leonardo da Vinci explains how to draw with this type of perspective:

6-14. Anna Mary Robertson (Grandma Moses). *Hoosick Falls, N.Y. in Winter.* Oil on masonite, 1944. (Permission The Phillips Collection, Washington, D.C.)

Of a mode of drawing a place accurately: Have a piece of glass as large as a half sheet of royal folio paper and set this firmly in front of your eyes, that is, between your eye and the thing you want to draw; then place yourself at a distance of two thirds of an ell from the glass, *fixing your head with a mechanism in such a way that you cannot move it at all.* Then *shut or cover one eye* and with a brush or drawing chalk draw upon the glass that which you see beyond it; then trace it on paper from the glass, afterward transfer it onto good paper, and paint it if you like . . . .[3]

Figure 6-16 shows a drawing mechanism based on this principle. What a strange way of looking at the world! A fixed, immovable head! A one-eyed view! Because of such rigid restrictions pure perspective drawings are generally mechanical and unappealing. Consequently, few artists—even realists—use the vanishing-point system in its pure form: rather, they soften and modify the system to reflect their own sensibilities.

With vanishing-point perspective the artist does not draw the world he knows but is involved instead in representing his retinal image as it might appear at a specific point in time in a specific location—a realistic approach in some ways but in other ways highly unrealistic. This perspective system makes sense only when the definition of realism is limited to duplication of the retinal image. The world we know and see is organized from an overwhelming bombardment of experiences and perceptions, including—but not limited to—the retinal image. The retinal image itself is in a constant state of flux—indeed, the retina ceases to respond in situations of unchanged stimulation (Chapter 7). The retinal image of a frozen instant of space/time represents an extremely minute portion of the total human visual experience.

Curiously, the break from retinal-image representation has been a painful, obstacle-ridden chapter in western art. Artists who reject this artificial vision have been heaped with public abuse. Labels like "primitive," "decorative," "avant-garde," "experimental," and "modern" have often been used as polite ways of separating certain types of art from "real" art. Terms such as "childish," "chaotic," "uncontrolled," and "decadent" are not so

6-15. (Photograph by the author.)

6-16. Albrecht Dürer. *Draftsman Drawing a Portrait.* Woodcut, 5 by 6 inches,c. 1525. (Permission Staatliche Museen, Preu–ßischer Kulturbesitz, Kupfer-Stichkabinett, Berlin.)

polite. Why are we locked into a system of evaluating and reacting to art according to a standard that limits artists to only one "correct" way of portraying reality?

The answer is complex. Not until the Renaissance did artists begin to make the distinction between the physical world and the visual field. The physical world is what you know: the true sizes of things, their true shapes, a Euclidean space where parallel lines never meet—a space more directly represented by isometric perspective (Chapter 5). The visual field, on the other hand, is what registers as the retinal image at any given instant. To understand why this distinction became important, we need to examine some of our traditions and values—philosophical commitments that began to coalesce and crystallize during the Italian Renaissance.

THE RENAISSANCE

The Renaissance (literally, "rebirth") was an awakening of learning and rationality following the mysticism and repression of the Middle Ages, when the human being was viewed as a miserable creature floundering adrift on the stormy sea of life, unable to control his fate except by religious ritual. In the Renaissance a new concept of the human being emerged—a strong and rational person, capable of discovering the truth about the universe, capable of controlling the world. Truth was no longer held to be a capricious gift from the Creator, a mystery that unfolded itself like a magic seed implanted in chosen individuals. Truth could be found by examining not the. soul but the physical world. The world could be explained objectively, rationally, impersonally: each person could separately discover, observe, and verify the truth; all individuals could understand it.

If truth does exist independently of individuals and is lying in wait to be discovered, then all persons will eventually arrive at the same truth. An observation must be true if it is found to be the same by separate individuals. In science this concept is called *replication*, and it is one of the foundations of scientific method. A scientific finding is recognized as valid if independent investigators are able to follow a given procedure and obtain the same results. Procedures that work for some experimenters but not for others are called *unscientific* and are held to be *invalid*, *unproven*, or *theoretical*. This method of dealing with reality is appealing, because it eliminates conflict and ambiguity by postulating that only one valid answer can exist. Replication is the means of proving whether or not the answer is correct.

Vanishing-point perspective fits neatly into this philosophy. It is consistent with the scientific method, for it can be replicated: any individual can go to the same location, hold his head in the same position, close the same eye, and see the same image in his visual field. Art produced in accordance with the vanishing-point system organizes a composition in relation to a specific location in time and space. This concept was to structure picture making and viewing for the next four hundred years: the picture plane as a window that looks out onto the world. Da Vinci describes it:

> . . . nothing else than seeing a place behind a pane of glass, quite transparent, on the surface of which objects behind the glass are drawn.[4]

This idea harmonizes with the idea of external truth, since such a vision can be imagined as existing on the glass independently of the individual looking at it.

CAMERA OBSCURA

In their enthusiasm for greater and greater accuracy in reproducing the visual field artists and scientists had to invent mechanical aids, since perception normally compensates for the deficiencies of the retinal image. One of the most widely used devices was the *camera obscura*. It was known by the Greeks as early as the fourth century B.C., although the earliest published drawing is dated 1544. The term literally translated from Italian means "dark room," and it derives from the discovery that if you make a small hole on the outside wall of a room, a small, inverted, and reversed image of the scene outside will be projected onto the opposite wall. This setup was wonderful for viewing solar eclipses, but for the artist it left much to be desired: only outdoor scenes could be projected, and the artist was limited to whatever was outside the wall, to working in the dark, and to the number of holes he was willing to make in the wall.

It is not surprising that by the 1600s portable box models had been developed and refined. Lenses were used to right the upside-down image and to adjust the focal point. Eventually, a slanted mirror was incorporated to reflect the image onto a translucent screen on top of the box (Figure 6-17).

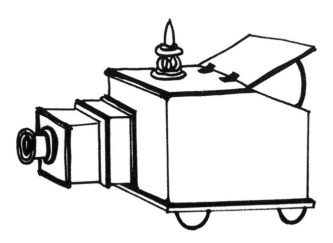

6-17. An early artist's camera obscura. (Adapted from *The Focal Encyclopedia of Photography* permission Focal Press, London and New York.)

These devices were fashionable with both serious and amateur artists until well into the last century. In the seventeenth century commercial exploitation of the perspective box produced traveling peep shows, a great popular entertainment of the day. In the eighteenth century coaches were occasionally transformed into traveling camera obscuras so that an artist could study the projected image of a scene without being exposed to the elements. A good deal of evidence indicates that the naturalistic effects painted by Jan Vermeer resulted from careful, accurate observation through a camera obscura (Figure 6-6).

Constant striving for accuracy in recording the projected image eventually led to experimentation with light-sensitive materials that could record the image independently of the prejudice of human vision. The ultimate outcome, of course, was the camera, which rendered the artist once and for all nonessential to the permanent, accurate reproduction of a projected image. It is no coincidence that the era in which the camera was invented and refined was the same era in which artists began to explore alternatives to the projected image as the only rightful concern of serious art. With the invention of the camera the artist was once again free to deal with personal visions and nonretinal aspects of reality. Liberated from the demand to interpret and reinterpret the visual field, artists over the past century have accomplished an astonishing variety of explorations into the content and materials of art. Movements have tumbled one after another into the public eye: impressionism, post-impressionism, fauvism, dada, futurism, cubism, surrealism, abstract expressionism, formalism; op, pop, minimal, and conceptual art.

But the general public has wanted art to be a mirror reflecting familiar images. To some viewers it has seemed as if the artist has walked away from his job. Looking for Beauty, they have often seen a Beast: ". . . a decorator tainted with insanity" (said of Gauguin); "an idiot . . . absolutely without talent . . . cut off from tradition . . . hopeless" (said of Cezanne); ". . . perfectly childish, crude and amateurish . . ." (said of Matisse); "an explosion in a shingle factory" (said of a painting by Duchamp); CUBISTS AND FUTURISTS MAKING INSANITY PAY (*The New York Times*).[5]

Traditional realism is comfortable because it portrays illusions of reality in a language that is already familiar. Traditions, in art as elsewhere, validate established ways of perceiving; they are reassuring. They reflect those aspects of the past that we have judged acceptable; they program our vision. The artist who goes against tradition is accused of not showing things "the way they're s'pozed to be."

But history shows us that art has always challenged the familiar scheme of things and has prophetically anticipated the very changes in consciousness that will later emerge. Artists continue to speculate, to explore, to hypothesize, to restructure perceptions, and to show us prophetic truths about ourselves and our times. For the viewer this is a disquieting challenge.

7. MOTION:

The Moving Picture

Is a lizard alive? Yes.

A nail? No.

A flower? No.

A tree? No.

Is the sun alive? Yes. Why? Because it moves when it has to.

Are the clouds alive? Yes, because they move and then they hit. What do they hit? They make the thunder when it rains.

Is the moon alive? Yes, because it moves.

The fire? Yes, because it crackles.

Is the wind alive? Yes, because on a windy day it's cold, it's always going faster.

A mountain? No, because it's always in the same place.

A motor? Yes, because it moves.

You know what it is to be alive? Yes, to move.[1]

For the child motion is magical, life-giving. His world is a field of movement, activity, spontaneous forces—life. Newborn infants—even before they can focus—follow moving objects with their eyes. And they are calmed by motion when they are rocked or carried. From birth humans respond to movement.

You arrive in the world with a physiology programmed for motion. The very functions and structures of your body require motion to maintain life. Without exercise your health declines; your metabolism becomes sluggish. Muscles atrophy from disuse. Just sitting too long in one position causes cramped muscles, stiff joints. Motion activates your nerve cells, gives you knowledge of yourself, tells you that you exist. Humans dread paralysis, the loss of motion, as a kind of death.

Freedom, our most cherished value, is defined in terms of motion:

. . . able to move in any direction, not held, as in chains, etc., not kept from motion, loose, not held or confined, unhindered, unhampered, not restricted by anything except its own limitations or nature . . .[2]

Those who would control us—whether for good or for ill—begin by controlling our movement:

Stay real close to Mommy, now.

Sit in your seat. Raise your hand if you need to leave the room. And sit still!

Atten-hut! Forward march! Left, right, left, right . . .

No running. No fishing. No hunting. No skating. No swimming. Do not walk on the grass.

Stop!

The language of motion expresses a variety of activities and experiences: consider such terms as e*motion*, de*motion*, pro*motion*, com*motion*, loco-*motion*.

PHYSIOLOGY

The perception of motion can be most simply defined as the perception of a succession of changes. The ability to detect motion is clearly an advantage in survival, since it is intimately related to perceiving both food and danger. The perception of motion is so basic that it appears to be innate and unlearned in human as well as other species.

Like your perception of light and sound, your perception of motion exists only within a limited range. Some motion is too slow to be seen, such as the movement of a minute hand on a watch or the opening of a flower. Some motion is too rapid to be seen, such as the change in frames on a motion-picture screen or the flicker of an incandescent light bulb. The range of motion to which humans are sensitive relates specifically to our survivial needs: it is important that we "see people and animals move from one place to the other; but we do not need to see the grass grow."[3]

Humans have evolved special physical structures to aid in the perception of motion. For instance, your eye muscles allow you to move your eyes up and down and side to side smoothly and rapidly. Your head can pivot nearly one hundred eighty degrees. With these structures it is physically possible for you to see objects within a three-hundred-sixty-degree field by moving only your head and eyes.

As an object moves across your visual field, the image travels across successive locations in the retina, and perception of motion results from a pattern of successive cell stimulation. When you keep a moving object in focus by moving your eyes and head, a feedback system also informs the brain of head and eye movement.

The retina itself actually *requires* change in the visual field in order to function. You can give your retina a pattern of unchanging stimulation by fixating on something (such as a speck on the wall) for a period of time. The image will fade, appear, and fade again periodically; the process may begin within five seconds. As the retinal cells adapt to the stimulus, they stop responding; following a rest period, partial sensitivity is recovered, then lost again as the cycle repeats itself. The continuous clarity of image which you normally experience is due at least partly to the rapid tremors or oscillations in the eye, which are continuously shifting the image onto fresh photoreceptors (see

Chapter 2). In this way your eye compensates for losses in sensitivity due to adaptation. You are definitely not structured for a static world!

The arrangement of rods and cones in the retina provides maximum acuity without sacrificing motion sensitivity. The concentration of cone cells toward the center of the retina (fovea) gives you greatest visual acuity in that area. But on the periphery of the retina the rods, which are highly sensitive to motion, predominate. You can perceive movement "out of the corner of your eye," even when you cannot identify *what* is moving (see the peripheral-vision experiment in Chapter 2). In addition, when motion registers in the periphery of the retina, it triggers a reflex that causes you to turn your head or eyes toward the source of the motion. The survival quotient is obvious: you can fixate on details in the center of the visual field and at the same time maintain a radarlike sensitivity to motion in the outer fringes of your vision. The head-turning reflex prompts you to react much faster than you could if you had to make a conscious decision.

Recent research shows that the brain as well as the eye contains specialized cells for motion detection. Two American physiologists (Hubel and Wiesel) conducted extensive experiments with electrodes that could monitor single brain cells in live cats. They observed some brain cells so specialized that they reacted *only* to movement and then only to movement in *a single direction!* Experiments with frogs have revealed similar cell specialization. Apparently, then, in the structuring of a perception individual cells operate in extremely limited and selective ways. Such findings are philosophical bombshells, since they present empirical evidence that we do not perceive reality directly—"as it is"—but rather that the only realities we *can* perceive are those made possible within the coding limitations of our neurophysiological structure.

THE STIMULUS
Motion attracts attention. Both humans and animals have strong and automatic reactions to motion. It is a stimulus of supreme importance, for it signals a change in the environment, a visible sign that some-

thing is happening—something you might need to react to.

Many, perhaps most, objects in your environment seem relatively unchanging. These inanimate objects may undergo changes over long periods of time or engage in motion on a molecular level unknown to your senses. But we do not term such changes "motion," because they are not visible: they cannot be seen by our eyes as a happening.

Motion perception occurs when you witness a series of visible changes. They can be changes in the shape or form of objects, changes in the spatial relationship among objects, or changes in the spatial relationship of yourself to the objects. All these changes involve visible *displacements* in space. Some displacements take place at such a rate that the succesive steps can be registered in the retina and relayed to the brain as they occur. This is *direct* or *simultaneous* perception of motion: as the motion occurs, corresponding activity occurs in your nervous system.

Sometimes spatial displacement is too fast to be seen, as in the case of a frog capturing an insect. Here the motion occurs at a rate too rapid for your nervous system to match. The motion is over before your eye and brain can register and process it. In other situations spatial displacements occur too slowly to be seen, as with the minute hand on a watch. If motion is very slow, the adaptation of the retinal cells occurs more rapidly than the motion, and the successive displacements register as stabilized images—not as activity. In both instances—motion that is too rapid or too slow—your perception of motion depends on experience and memory and not on matching nervous-system activity. This is *indirect* or *inferred* perception of motion.

FRAME OF REFERENCE
You commonly perceive an object moving against a background. You see a person walking across a room or an automobile moving along a highway. As the object moves, you see it change location in relation to its surroundings. The background is a *frame of reference* against which you can measure the object's displacement. Because of this basic experience you operate on the general rule that a *figure moves and the background stands still.* Occasionally this assumption misleads you: for instance, when you see scudding clouds moving in front of the moon. You tend to see the moon moving, because the moon is normally perceived as a figure.

This perceptual prejudice is more suited to primitive lifestyles in which the environment does not move. For this reason modern locomotion has its disconcerting moments. Perhaps you have been on a train or subway when a train on an adjoining track began to move—for a moment you think your own train has started up. This happens because when you see a window, the scene beyond it is perceptually organized as a ground. When the ground changes, you automatically assume that you are moving, since backgrounds normally stand still. Witkin's tilting-room experiments (Chapter 5) played with this assumption by moving a subject's entire environment. At the same time the experimenters withheld cross-checking data that would normally be available in a real-life situation (e.g., the subway). For some subjects the illusion was so strong that they felt as if they were falling off the chair.

Momentary disorientation can also occur in relation to a large body of water. When you stand on a dock, you may have the sensation that you are slowly drifting away. Here the fixated object operates as a figure, and the nonfixated part of the visual field is a ground. When you fixate on the dock you see it as a figure moving against the background of the water. But when you fixate on the water, the perception becomes correct.

Perception of speed and velocity depends to a great extent on the relation of object to background. A small object in a large field seems to move much more slowly than a large object in a small field. When you watch airplanes flying at high altitudes, you may find it difficult to comprehend the extreme speed at which the plane is moving. The size of the plane's image in relation to the huge expanse of sky makes the velocity of the plane appear to be very slow.

An object moving across a homogeneous background seems to move at a slower speed than an object moving across a variegated background. A background with variety provides more stationary reference points and therefore reminds you continuously that motion is taking place. This is another reason why airplanes seem to move slowly: the sky is a uniform background with few points of **reference for motion. For this reason aircraft may** seem to move more rapidly on a clear, starry night than on a clear day. The same effect can occur on land, too. I traveled by automobile to the midwestern plains after living several years in a hilly landscape. On the Kansas turnpike the areas of sky and land are so vast that the displacement of automobiles in relation to the landscape seems to occur much more slowly. I felt as if I were moving about forty miles an hour, although the speedometer was registering eighty!

Some observers have defined a *hierarchy of dependence* in the visual field. According to this concept, when you spontaneously organize a perception of the visual field, you automatically assign to some objects the role of a dominant framework upon which other objects are dependent. For example, "The room serves as framework for the table, the table for the fruit bowl, the fruit bowl for the apples."[4] This hierarchy is basically equivalent to figure/ground relationships, which shift according to where you focus attention. The dependence concept, however, is convenient to use when discussing motion, since it is easy to think of object motion in relation to constant or fixed frameworks. Using the hierarchy of dependence, you can predict what will be seen as moving and what will be seen as stationary in perceptual situations in which you withhold normal data for cross-checking within a general frame of reference. The following relationships may be of practical interest to readers involved in projects such as film animation, light shows, visual training, and perception experiments:

1. The figure tends to be seen as moving, and the framework or ground as stationary when a displacement occurs.

2. Objects that are variable (i.e., undergo changes in size or shape) tend to be seen as moving in relation to objects that remain constant.

3. When two objects close to each other are displaced, the smaller object will be seen as moving.

4. Where there is a difference in brightness, the dimmer object appears to move when displacement takes place.

5. A fixated object assumes the character of a figure and thus tends to be seen as moving, while a nonfixated or blurred portion of the field assumes the role of a stationary ground.

THE OBSERVER

When you move your head or body, you change the spatial relationship between your eyes and the environment, which causes corresponding changes in your visual field (*motion parallax*). These changes are a type of gradient: a sequence of changing spatial displacements that give a perception of space and motion. Like other perceptual gradients, motion parallax is an artifact of the visual field and therefore provides data that is relevant only to the observer's unique frame of reference.

You perceive even time in relation to yourself. You learn to measure time by experiencing how long it takes to make certain movements and by observing events taking place. Perceptions of time come from your stored memories of motion and change. Measures of time within your own mind can be very personal—unrelated to clock time. When you are really engrossed in what you are doing, hours seem to fly by in minutes. Sleep studies show that the motion experienced during dreams actually takes place within seconds, although to the dreamer it seems to last much longer. During a sudden trauma the opposite is sometimes true. An automobile accident may be experienced with a sensation of slow motion—each detail perceived with crystal clarity—even though the whole sequence takes place in the twinkling of an eye. With the invention of clocks people became less dependent on subjective measures of time. Clocks measure time intervals objectively, independently of the significance of events.

ILLUSIONS OF MOTION

You perceive motion when you perceive either of these conditions:

1. Displacement in space occurring in successive steps (direct or simultaneous perception of motion).

2. Change in conditions such that you conclude

that motion has taken place (indirect or inferred perception of motion).

You can be fooled if your eyes encounter non-moving stimuli that correspond to either of these conditions. An illusion of motion will seem as real as actual motion as long as the image stimulation is the same.

PERSISTENCE OF VISION

A familiar illusion of motion is produced in the "flip" book, in which a series of pictures is shown rapidly to the eye: slight changes from picture to picture represent changes in position or location (*animation* or *serial transformation*). As you flip the pages, the illusion of motion is quite compelling.

This effect of motion is due to a phenomenon called *persistence of vision*, which means that image stimulation continues in the retina for a fraction of a second beyond the initial exposure to the stimulus (*retinal lag*). Thus, when separate similar images are shown very rapidly, the retinal stimulations merge into one another, and the image is experienced as continuous.

A dramatic demonstration of this phenomenon was made around 1825 by the English scientist Michael Faraday. Faraday masked a pattern with an opaque cardboard disk that had a single narrow slit in it. When the disk was rotated, the *entire* pattern behind the disk could be seen (Figure 7-1). You notice the same effect with a large fan when it is turned on: you can see "through" the blades of the fan while they are moving. When tiny fragments of an image are seen in rapid enough succession, they are perceived as a whole image—in spite of the fact that at any given instant all but a fraction of the image is masked!

Persistence of vision was observed as early as the first century B.C. and was mentioned by Ptolemy and da Vinci. Surprisingly, the principle did not capture the popular imagination until the early 1800s, when a number of toys and entertainments based on this phenomenon appeared. One of the simplest, known as a thaumatrope, consisted of a disk with a picture printed on each side and two strings attached for twirling the disk between the thumb and forefinger. When the disk was rotated, the two pictures merged into one (Figure 7-2).

Another popular toy was the zoetrope (known also as the daedalum or wheel of life), a revolving metal drum pierced with thin slots. A paper strip showing phases of movement (e.g., a juggler or a seagull skimming the water) was inserted into the drum, and the figures were viewed through the slots while the drum was rotated (Figure 7-3). Similar toys are occasionally reproduced by modern manufacturers.

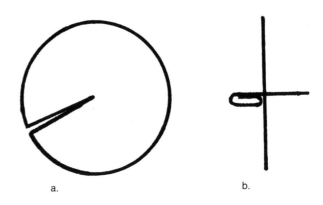

a.   b.

7-1. (a.) To make a Faraday disk from lightweight cardboard, cut a circle about six inches in diameter with a very narrow slit. (b.) Spin it on a shaft made from a bent paper clip. While the disk is in motion, you can see everything behind it.

7-2. Front and back of thaumatrope disk. (British Crown Copyright, Science Museum, London.)

MOTION, PICTURES, AND MOTION PICTURES

In the late 1800s Eadweard Muybridge became interested in proving whether or not all four feet of a moving horse are ever off the ground at the same time—an issue that had been argued as far back as ancient Egypt. Muybridge set up a series of timed cameras, and the resulting photographs revealed

7-3. Zoetrope. (British Crown Copyright. Science Museum, London.)

7-4. Eadweard Muybridge. *Horse Galloping: Daisy with Rider* (plate 67). (Reproduced from *Animals in Motion* by Eadweard Muybridge, reprinted in 1957 by Dover Publications, New York.) Exposures 7 and 8 clearly show the horse's feet off the ground.

that during certain phases of the horse's stride all four feet were indeed off the ground! The photographs were published in magazines and journals of the time, including *Scientific American* (Figure 7-4).[5]

Today it is difficult for us to appreciate the great excitement and controversy that surrounded the photographs by Muybridge and others. We must remind ourselves that certain aspects of human and animal motion simply had never before been seen by the human eye, because they occur too rapidly. Until this time artists and illustrators had depended on certain accepted conventions or formulas for showing motion. A galloping horse, for example, was shown with front legs stretched forward and hind legs backward. But Muybridge's photos clearly showed that when all four feet were off the ground, they were bunched together under the horse's belly! Compared to the familiar schemata of the artist, the photographs looked unreal. One observer remarked, "No artist would have dared to draw a . . . figure in attitudes like some of these."[6]

Muybridge decided to conduct more extensive studies of motion. He used between ten and forty cameras at once, some with multiple lenses triggered by an electromagnetic shutter device of his own invention that could be set for predetermined time intervals. Eventually he produced more than 100,000 photographic plates containing more than 20,000 figures of moving humans and animals.

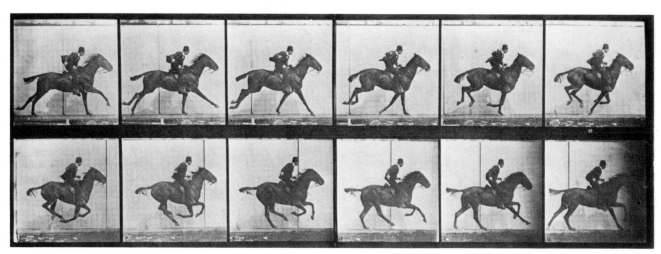

He intended "to create an atlas for the use of artists, a visual dictionary of human and animal forms in action."[7] Although some of the photographs now seem quaint, these volumes remain a standard practical reference for phases of motion and continue to be used by many artists today.

Muybridge also experimented with the zoetrope, making his own photo sequences as well as stereoscopic pictures from twin-lens cameras. He was able to produce a convincing illusion of a solid miniature horse trotting and galloping. In 1888 Muybridge consulted with Thomas Edison about the possibility of using his version of the zoetrope in conjunction with the phonograph in order to reproduce action simultaneously with words. The scheme was temporarily abandoned, but in 1898 Muybridge speculated:

> The combination of such an instrument with the phonograph has not, at the time of writing, been satisfactorily accomplished; there can, however, be but little doubt that in the—perhaps not far distant—future, instruments will be constructed that will not only reproduce visible actions simultaneously with audible words, but an entire opera, with the gestures, facial expressions, and songs of the performers, with all the accompanying music, will be recorded and reproduced ... for the instruction or entertainment of an audience ... and if the photographs should have been made stereoscopically, and projections from each series be independently and synchronously projected on a screen, a perfectly realistic imitation of the original performance will be seen . . . by the use of properly constructed binocular glasses.[8]

Muybridge had anticipated talking motion pictures by thirty years and 3-D movies by nealy sixty years!

A movie film is made up of a series of *frames* or still pictures. As in the flip book, each picture represents a slight change from the preceding one. Early motion-picture cameras photographed fewer frames per second than do modern movie cameras. This means that fewer successive images were used to portray a certain movement, and the transitions from frame to frame were less smooth. Phases of very rapid movements could occur *in between* frames and thus fail to be recorded on film at all! Under these conditions the projected motion appears speeded up, jerky, and awkward—effects that contribute to the comic qualities of early silent films. Slow motion in films is produced by exposing *more* frames per second than normal and then projecting the film at normal speed. Transitions between frames are extremely smooth, and the effect is one of great ease and fluidity.

CRITICAL FUSION FREQUENCY

A noticeable characteristic of early motion pictures was their flickering quality. When a motion picture is projected, the light is on only while a frame is actually being projected onto the screen: the light is off during the transition between frames. The on-off cycle in the early projector light was slow enough for viewers to be aware of a definite flicker. Hence, early movies were commonly called "the flicks." The flicker effect still exists in movie projection, but now it takes place at a rate of seventy-two flashes per second. This is too rapid for you to perceive the separate flashes, so the light appears to be steady. The point at which you will perceive a flashing light as steady occurs between thirty and fifty flashes per second, depending on the brightness of the light. This point is called the *critical fusion frequency*.

Critical fusion frequency demonstrates once again the limits on your ability to perceive reality. If your eyes were perfectly accurate, the retinal stimulation would correspond exactly to the time length of the stimulus, and you could see the on-off flashes. Because of retinal lag (or persistence of vision), stimulation in the retina lasts *longer* than the light stimulus, and the separate stimulations merge into a continuous sensation. Without this fusion point, you might live in a strange world. For example, incandescent light bulbs, which operate on alternating current, actually flicker at a rate of sixty cycles per second. Because this is above the critical fusion frequency, however, you perceive a steady light. The flicker rate of fluorescent lights is somewhat lower and often can be detected in peripheral vision, where your eye is more sensitive to motion.

Low-frequency flicker can interfere with brain

functions. Stimulation by bright, flashing lights (such as strobes) at a rate of about four to ten flashes per second can cause people to experience strange visual patterns, headache, and nausea. People with a tendency to epilepsy sometimes suffer convulsions due to flicker in the environment from such things as television, the rotor blades of a helicopter, or flickering sunlight.

PHI PHENOMENON

When you look at flip books, motion pictures, and television, you are seeing *apparent* movement. You perceive movement where none exists because the successive images are similar and close together in location. The perception of apparent movement has been investigated by laboratory experiments in which the subject is placed in a dark room and shown two lights, one of which goes on when the other one goes off. If the lights are fairly close together and the on-off interval is right, the subject perceives the stimulus as a single light moving from one location to the other. This apparent movement, called the *phi phenomenon*, is frequently used in commercial signs and marquees: single lights are flashed on and off in succession, giving the impression of a moving image such as an arrow.

The effect of the phi phenomenon is strengthened by persistence of vision, which encourages the fusion of successive images, and also by your basic tendency to group together into a meaningful whole stimuli that are similar in form and location (see Chapter 3). As with all illusions, the input is identical to that from a "real" stimulus, and you can recognize the stimulus as an illusion only by cross-checking with other available data.

WATERFALL EFFECT

Try looking steadily at the center of a moving phonograph record, then suddenly stop the turntable. For several seconds it will seem as if the record is going around in the opposite direction. The same effect can be experienced if you watch flowing water such as a river, then look at a fixed object such as the bank: it will seem to be flowing in a direction opposite to that of the water. This illusion of motion, documented as far back as Aristotle, is known as the *waterfall effect* or the *aftereffect of seen movement*.

Figure 7-5 shows two standard patterns for demonstrating this phenomenon. When the spiral pattern is rotated so that it seems to be expanding, it will seem to be contracting when the motion is stopped (or vice versa, depending on the direction of rotation). The same effect occurs with the single radial line.

Just why the waterfall effect occurs is not clear. Some theories suggest that it results from overload firing of the specialized cell circuits in the brain that respond to motion. Other researchers feel that adaptation processes in the retina are at least partly responsible. In any case a stationary reference within the visual field appears essential for the waterfall effect to occur. This illusion, fortunately, does not happen when the moving field covers the entire retina. If it did, we would suffer the waterfall illusion at every sudden automobile stop!

7-5. To make your own demonstrations of the waterfall effect, copy the patterns with Magic Markers onto circles of lightweight cardboard about six inches in diameter. Spin the disks as shown in Figure 7-1b.

AUTOKINETIC MOVEMENT

You might call this effect the Case of the Wandering Spot. If you can find a completely dark room, place yourself at one end, and at the other end place a small point of light, such as a lighted cigarette on an ashtray or a flashlight in a lightproof box pierced with a small nail hole. After you gaze at the light for a few seconds, it will appear to wander about in a rather erratic manner. If you introduce more spots, they will stabilize in relation to one another, but the entire constellation may go into autokinetic motion and seem to move about. Theories vary as to the exact cause of this peculiar perception, but in any event the phenomenon provides additional evidence of the requirement for reference points in the visual field: the illusion disappears as soon as the observer is able to perceive his position in relation to a visible, stationary object.

MOTION IN ART

From the cradle to the grave we entertain ourselves with motion: jointed dolls, jack-in-the-boxes, spinning tops, limber jacks, gyroscopes, kaleidoscopes, electric trains, pecking chickens on a paddle, shoe-button eyes, tropical fish, wind-up toys, carnival rides, pinball machines, kites, spitballs, push toys, pull toys, sports cars, dangly earrings, ant farms, home movies, porch swings, waterbeds, television, and rocking chairs. Perhaps we never totally lose the childhood sensibility that equates motion with life.

Motion has long been an element of popular entertainment and folk art—the art of ordinary people. Folk art is popular, easily understood, and often created anonymously. The wind is used as a natural energy source to generate motion in folk-art forms such as weather vanes, the famous Japanese kites, and the whimsical whirligig, which apparently originated in Europe (Figure 7-6).

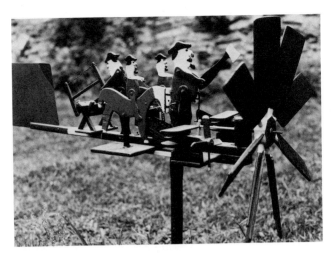

7-6. Whirligig. (Permission Agathe Walter, Willimantic, Connecticut.)

As with other art forms, folk art often involves generations of custom and craftsmanship. Both the Near and the Far East have centuries-old traditions of shadow puppets, which are elegant in decoration and highly sophisticated in movement and story-telling. In some Eastern countries, particularly India, Thailand, and Java, shadow puppets are so seriously regarded that women are not allowed to look upon their faces! Europe also has a rich heritage of puppets and marionettes—Punch and Judy are only two of many classic characters.

A standard we commonly apply to fine art is its timelessness, its constancy, its unchanging qualities. Objects of art have been traditionally considered to exist outside the dimension of time and because of this to have a certain immortality. A major function of museums is to preserve artworks from suffering change through deterioration or vandalism.

While paintings and sculpture often portray motion, they are themselves motionless. We frequently speak of a painting or sculpture as representing a "frozen instant" of time. Over the centuries artists have explored various ways of giving static art forms a sense of life and motion. It is often hard to figure out exactly why some paintings and sculptures seem to come alive, while others seem dead and lifeless.

An art object that does not itself move cannot give you a direct perception of motion: inferred motion is the most that you can expect. A two-dimensional artist, then, must structure his work in such a way that you can perceive imagined movement. Some artists achieve this by representing an action not at its climax but at a point a few moments earlier so that the imagination of the viewer will complete or "fill in" the motion (Figure 7-7). This approach has been called the *pregnant moment* or *directed tension*. It seems to be consistent with the Gestalt principle that perception will organize the best form consistent with the data (see Chapters 1 and 3). When a stimulus deviates from a norm, added perceptual energy is required to correct it, and greater tension release accompanies closure. If the frustration has not been too great, the "reward" value of the closure is greater, and the perception is dynamic and self-reinforcing.

The pregnant moment is a way of portraying a deviation from a norm category and results in a more dynamic perception than would be given by the norm stimulus itself.

Objects may also be portrayed with enough ambiguity for several phases of motion to be perceived in a single image. A common way of doing this is to blur the edge of an object represented as moving. This method is effective because when you perceive a real moving object, you cannot clearly define its edge—the edge is constantly changing location. An example of this technique is a picture of a stagecoach with blurry wheels and spokes.

A subtler way of filling a painting with apparent movement can be seen in the work of the medieval painter Giotto (Figure 7-8). Giotto portrayed phases of motion in a sequence that moves from image to image. If you look at the figures in the composition sequentially, you will see that the transition from one to another is rather like a serial transformation. Serial transformation is effective for the same reason as the phi phenomenon: we connect a sequence of images that are similar in form and close together in location. Such perceptions of motion in paintings are for the most part unconscious, so the painting seems to have a quality of dynamic mystery. Serial transformation has been used by other artists, such as Matisse (Figure 7-9).

Another way of showing motion in painting is to expose the *process* of painting in the work. In Zen brush painting (Figure 3-15) the integrity of the brushstrokes is emphasized: a brushstroke must reveal how fully the brush was loaded, in what direction it was moved, how much pressure was used, and how fast it was drawn across the paper. In the oriental tradition the brushstroke becomes a record of motion, a "footprint" of the energy that created it.

7-7. Peter Paul Rubens. *Descent fom the Cross.* Oil on panel, 156 by 121 inches, 1612. (Permission Notre-Dame Cathedral, Antwerp.)

7-8. Giotto. *Pieta.* Fresco, 1305. (Permission Cappela Degli Scrovegni, Padua.)

7-9. Henri Matisse. *Dance* (first version). Oil on canvas, 102½ by 153½ inches, 1909. (Collection The Museum of Modern Art, New York. Gift of Nelson A. Rockefeller in honor of Alfred H. Barr, Jr.)

7-10. Peter MacLean. *Arrangement: 100 square feet tar paper to 100 square feet floor.* Floorspace 10 feet by 10 feet, tar paper 3 feet by 33 feet 4 inches, 1973. (Permission of the artist.)

Often the character of the brushstroke expresses particular energies associated with the subject of the painting. This value system contrasts sharply with the traditional western view that brushstrokes should not show.

The action painters and abstract expressionists of the 1930s and 1940s had a philosophy similar to the Zen painters, although their work is much more abstract. Jackson Pollock, Franz Kline, and Willem de Kooning, rebelling against traditional illusionism, felt that the process and movement involved in the act of painting should be revealed—not hidden—in the finished work. When you look at the works of these painters (Figure C-8), you may react strongly to the energy of their creation: seeing visible, aggressive brushstrokes on a canvas—if you are used to "invisible" brushwork—can be quite shocking. When these paintings were first shown, public reaction was extremely negative, and the painters became the object of ridicule. Pollock, in fact, was dubbed "Jack the Dripper."

Some of today's conceptual artists also believe that an artwork should reveal how it was made. Unlike expressionist work, however, the experience is not emotional, but rather an intellectual involvement in which the viewer can imagine step-by-step the moves by which the artist constructed the object (Figure 7-10).

Optical techniques are yet another approach to showing movement in painting. Painted surfaces may seem to dance and shimmer uncontrollably as a result of afterimages, groupings, color vibrations, or other optical phenomena (Figures 2-8, 2-14, 3-17, C-1, and C-9).

THE MOVING VIEWER

Sculptors have always worked closely with the concrete aspects of motion, for a sculpture exists in three-dimensional space. Although it does not move, the viewer does: unlike a painting, a sculpture does not require that you stand in one place to see it. The perception of a sculpture is organized from successive views experienced through time (Figure 7-11). The totality of a sculpture is like the totality of a piece of music: no single note reveals the whole—the parts must be experienced through sequence and time.

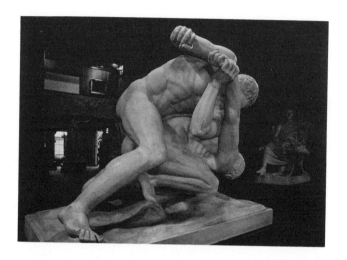

7-11. *The Wrestlers.* Greek, 3rd to 1st century B.C. Plaster cast from the original in the Uffizzi Gallery, Florence. (Permission Slater Memorial Museum, Norwich, Connecticut. Photograph by Bruce Thompson.)

Since the turn of the century artists have become increasingly involved with the motion of the viewer. Optical artists introduced a variety of relief constructions using such elements as multiple planes, modular units, and transparent layers (Figure 7-12). What you see depends on your location in space: the artwork springs to life with each movement you make. The current trend toward environments involves the moving viewer as an active participant. You can actually enter a large-scale construction and move through a sequence of perceptual situations created by the artist. The purpose of most environments is to give you an intensely personal perceptual experience.

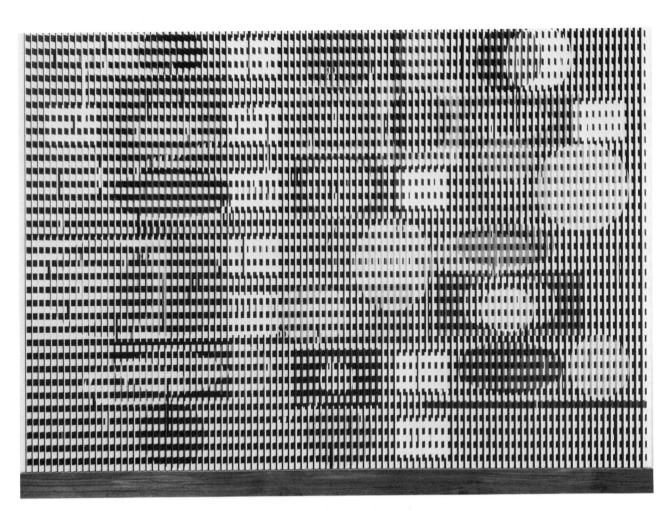

7-12. AGAM (Yaacov Agam). *Double Metamorphosis II*. Oil on aluminum, 106 by 158 inches. (Collection The Museum of Modern Art, New York. Gift of Mr. and Mrs. George M. Jaffin.)

THE MOVING ARTWORK

Although other artists had experimented with moving structures, Alexander Calder succeeded in capturing the imagination of the public with his mobiles. In the 1930s Calder began producing sculptures of abstract shapes, delicately balanced and hinged to move gracefully in chain reactions and to respond to slight movements of the surrounding air (Figure 7-13). Mobiles are only one type of *kinetic sculpture*, as moving artworks are sometimes called. Using the concept of an artwork moving through time and space in combination with modern technology, present-day artists work with motorized movement, electromagnetic fields, sound-activated structures, light, and many other materials.

The traditional unmoving picture plane with its "frozen slices" of time has become increasingly inadequate for many artists. The visual artist is concerned more and more with sophisticated issues arising from the fundamental nature of time, space, change, force, and energy and how we perceive them.

7-13. Alexander Calder. *Sumac.* Steel wire and painted sheet metal, 49¾ by 94 inches, 1961. (Permission Mr. and Mrs. David Lloyd Kreeger, Washington, D.C. Photograph permission Perls Gallery, New York.)

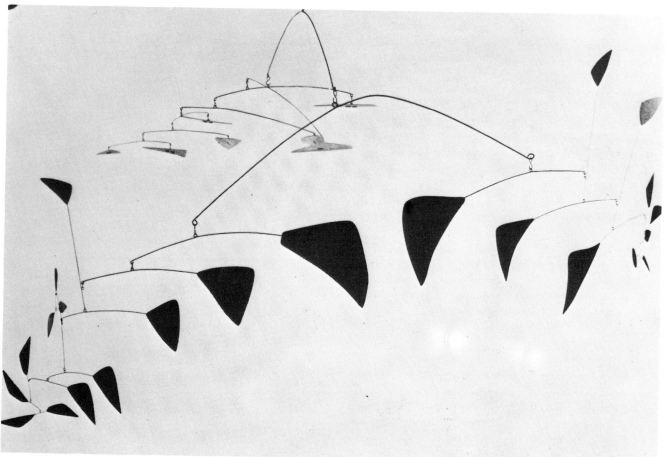

8. COLOR:

It's All Relative

Have you ever been green with envy? Turned red as a beet? Thought someone else was yellow? Felt blue? Become white as a sheet? Our language patterns reveal an emotionally charged relationship to color. When you stop to think about it, the delineation between *black and white* and *color* is a very odd division in our visual experience. Black-and-white images in photographs, movies, and television indicate that the dimension of color can be completely removed from some situations without affecting our ability to perceive visual information. On the other hand, there is practically no market for black-and-white home-movie film—which shows that for most people color is a profoundly important dimension of personal experience.

In spite of this basic human response to color, science has yet to unlock many mysteries about our color vision. Of all the perceptual processes discussed in this book, color vision is the most problematic and the least understood.

WHAT IS COLOR?
Colors are component parts of light, the portion of the electromagnetic spectrum to which your eyes respond (Figure 2-4). You perceive differences in light frequencies just as you perceive differences in sound frequencies. Different frequencies of sound are experienced as differences in pitch. Different frequencies of light are experienced as dif-

ferences in color. The color range that you can perceive extends from red (the longest visible wavelength) to violet (the shortest visible wavelength). When a beam of light is spread out, or *diffracted*, through a prism, various frequencies are visible as an ordered arrangement of color, the *spectrum*. After a rain droplets of moisture in the air act as diffractors, and you see a rainbow. The light frequencies actually exist in a continuum, but ordinarily seven spectral zones are identified separately by name: red, orange, yellow, green, blue, indigo, and violet. (ROY G. BIV is a memory aid for the spectral order.)

In general, objects that are not light sources are light reflectors. Their surfaces absorb, or subtract out a portion of the light wave, and reflect back another portion. This reflected light is the objective stimulus we call color. For example, green leaves reflect the green portion of the light spectrum. The mixing of pigments (as in paints or dyes) is a subtractive process. Color in light, on the other hand, is additive, for when all frequencies are united, the result is a white light in which the colors are not visible as separate entities.

THE EYE
The fact that you can see color means that the photoreceptors in the retina are able in some way to differentiate among the various wave fre-

quencies of light. Since you do not see color at night (rod vision) but you do see color in daylight (cone vision), color perception must occur in the cone cells. The average person can distinguish between one hundred thirty and two hundred separate colors. Since there are not one or two hundred different types of photoreceptors, color must be perceived through coding combinations among a few basic types of receptors.

One major theory of color vision, the Young-Helmholtz theory, postulates three types of color receptors, each having a heightened sensitivity to a specific color: red, green, or blue. This is called the *trichromatic* or *three-receptor theory*. The perception of other colors is explained as the result of mixes among the three types of receptors. Color blindness is thought to result from dysfunction in certain types of receptors.

The Young-Helmholtz theory does not easily explain why people tend to perceive four colors as fundamental and unique: blue, green, yellow, and red. Further, these basic colors are paired in vision in specific ways: red with green, and blue with yellow. Members of these pairs do not blend: for example, we cannot think of a reddish green or yellowish blue. The paired colors also trigger responses to each other: neutral gray looks pinkish when surrounded by green, and greenish when surrounded by red. Yellow and blue also have a reciprocal or *complementary* relationship. Afterimages show that these pairs have some intimate relationship within the retina: a negative afterimage appears in colors that are paired complements to the stimulus image (Figure C-2).

Another explanation, the Hering theory, also postulates three types of receptors but describes the three types as red-green, yellow-blue, and black-white receptors. The response capabilities are mutually exclusive: that is, a single receptor can actively signal only one response *or* the other. According to this theory negative afterimages occor because the complementary response is electrochemically àctive, while the receptor returns to a state of normal sensitivity. The Hering theory seems to explain the existence of four seemingly fundamental colors more simply and also to account for reciprocal relationships between paired

colors in both afterimages and color blindness.

Despite the plausibility of these theories, researchers continue to encounter evidence that does not fit, and the precise mechanism of color vision remains open to speculation.

THE BRAIN

If we know little about what happens in the retina, we know even less about how color stimulations are processed by the brain. Recent experiments by Edwin Land, inventor of the Polaroid Land camera, have raised a great many questions about the nature of color perception. Land has been able to project onto a screen images in which colors appear that are *not physically present* in either the transparencies or the filters involved! He has also demonstrated that in identical frequencies a greater range of color is perceived when a pattern is complex than when it is simple. And further, the colors that are seen depend on whether or not the light patterns are perceived as representing objects! While it is not possible to discuss the Land experiments in detail here, they have clearly demonstrated that wavelengths alone do not determine color perception. As with other aspects of vision, the retina proves to be only a starting point for complex internal events in which sensory stimulation is mysteriously transformed and transmuted into comprehensible perceptions.

CONTEXT

Context is the most influential frame of reference for color perception. A single swatch of color will seem brighter, duller, lighter, darker, or changed in hue—by changing only the context in which the color is seen (Figure C-3). You have probably experienced this apparent fickleness of color. A chair, rug, or paint color selected in the environment of a store may appear surprisingly different in the color context of your own home. A scarf, belt, or sweater may seem garish and harsh with some color combinations but harmonious with others. Artists and designers in the fields of fashion, textiles, interior design, and advertising are constantly confronted with such delicate balances in color relationships. According to Josef Albers, the well-known artist and teacher, "...no normal eye, not even the most trained one, is foolproof against color deception. He who claims to see colors independent of their illusionary changes fools only himself. . . ."[1]

CONSTANCY
The principle of constancy dominates color perception as dramatically as it governs the perception of size. You experience the colors of objects in different situations of context and illumination, and from these experiences you structure mental norms that define the "real" color of an object. A color constant is sometimes called *object color* or *local color:* a notion of the "normal" color of something, independent of the effects of illumination and shadow (grass is green, tree trunks are brown, sidewalks are gray, apples are red, etc.). This saves you the energy and effort of continually processing the data at hand, but it also keeps you from seeing the actual color variability in your environment and causes you instead to see the colors you expect to see. In one experiment subjects were shown two shapes, a leaf and a donkey. Both shapes were colored an identical greenish-brown, but subjects reported the leaf shape as green and the donkey shape as brown!

Constancy may have a particularly important function in the case of color, since we have very poor color memory. Most people encounter great difficulty even in matching colors they have seen innumerable times. Extreme error is common when a person tries to match a paint sample or a piece of clothing from memory alone.

Color constancy discounts shadow effects. For this reason you may mistakenly regard shadows caused by the interruption of light as black. Beginning artists often express this perception by coloring shadows gray or black. In fact, shadow color results from the interaction of several factors: the predominant and complementary colors of the illumination, the object color, and the subtle reflections of color from nearby surfaces. You can experience more accurate color perception by looking at surfaces and shadows through a narrow tube or a hole in the center of a blank card. This allows you to isolate a color area from its surroundings and from the boundaries of objects. An artist who wishes to paint the natural appearances of objects must painstakingly train himself to see things in this way.

COLOR TERMINOLOGY
Color is traditionally said to have three dimensions: hue, value, and intensity. *Hue* refers to the basic name of the color (blue, turquoise, magenta, yellow, etc.).

Value refers to the lightness or darkness of the color as it corresponds to a scale of grays ranging between white and black. You can think of value as the shade of gray that the color would register if it were photographed in black and white. Not all hues have the same range of values. Yellow, for instance, is basically quite light in value: darkening yellow will drastically alter its identity—a really dark value of yellow is more like the color of mud. Red, blue, and purple have basically dark values. Red cannot be significantly lightened without losing its basic quality of redness and turning into pink. Blue and violet are not so subject to this kind of change. *Tints* are lighter than normal values of color (e.g., pink, baby blue, light green). *Shades* are darker than normal values (e.g., deep purple, dark green).

Intensity refers to the purity, brilliance, or saturation of the color. A high-intensity green, for example, is the purest, most brilliant green possible. A color that results from a mixture of hues is always less intense than any of the component colors. This phenomenon has practical implications, especially for artists. For instance, if you want a very intense color, you should buy it ready-made, because any color you mix will have less intensity than the parent colors. You can also tone down an intense color without muddying it by mixing in another color (not black); a good way to do this is to add a touch of the complementary color. Inexperienced people sometimes try to tone down a color by adding black and are disappointed when the color becomes unattractive.

THE COLOR WHEEL
Art students have traditionally learned how pigment colors are related to one another by means of the color wheel (Figure 8-1). The function of the

color wheel is to demonstrate certain color relationships. The colors are arranged in spectral order, with the high and low ends (red and violet) adjacent to one another. The three *primary* colors (which cannot be mixed from other colors) red, yellow, and blue, are placed equidistantly apart. The *secondary* colors, orange, green, and violet, are placed between the primaries from which they are mixed. *Tertiary* colors (yellow-orange, yellow-green, blue-green, blue-violet, red-violet, and red-orange) are mixed from adjacent primary and secondary colors.

Colors opposite one another on the color wheel are complements. The complement of each primary color is the secondary color mixed from the other two primaries. Because any complementary pairs always contain, between the two of them, all three primary colors, they produce black when mixed together.

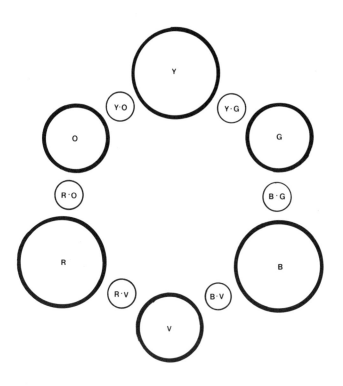

8-1. Color wheel.

COLOR SCHEMES
Monochromatic (one-color) schemes use one hue, with variations in value and/or intensity.

Analogous schemes use three to five hues that are adjacent to one another on the color wheel and contain a hue in common—for example, yellow-green, yellow, and yellow-orange.

Complementary schemes use adjacent hues with their respective complements.

Split-complementary schemes are based on one hue and two colors on either side of the complement—for example, blue with yellow-orange and red-orange.

Triad schemes involve any three hues equidistant from one another on the color wheel.

Tetrad schemes involve any four hues equidistant from one another on the color wheel.

The color wheel and other color structures can supply a helpful vocabulary for articulating order and relationship among colors, but relying too much on such formulas will keep you from being alert to your own perceptions. In the past color-wheel recipes provided a standard method of color selection in fields such as interior decoration, textile design, and fashion. However, the contemporary emphasis on individuality and variety encourages people to experiment and to trust their own sensibilities rather than conforming to rigid conventions. Art students are also becoming more involved with empirical experimentation and the development of perceptual sensitivity.

PERCEPTUAL COLOR
SUCCESSIVE CONTRAST
In the afterimage experience (Figure C-2) intense exposure to one color results in the sensation of its complement when the stimulus is withdrawn. Because the contrasting experience of the complement follows the perception of the stimulus color, it is called *successive contrast*.

SIMULTANEOUS CONTRAST
Complementary-color effects occur not only after viewing but during viewing, because the stimulus color simultaneously generates subtle sensations of its opposite. For example, a gray circle on a green background will appear slightly pinkish.

The presence of blue will enhance the orange aspects of a red; conversely, the red will bring out greenish qualities in the blue. In this way the apparent contrast between the colors is perceptually increased. Because this effect occurs during exposure to the color stimulus, it is called *simultaneous contrast*. When complementary colors are seen together, the simultaneous-contrast effect is at a maximum, and the combination may seem uncomfortably bold (e.g., red and green, blue and orange).

Simultaneous contrast also occurs with respect to values. A middle-value gray will look darker on a white background and lighter on a black background (Figure 8-2). Since colors have values, the perceived value of a color, as well as its perceived hue, is affected by the surrounding color (Figure C-3).

The rule is: the perception of a color is affected in the direction of the complementary hue and value of the color around it. Bright, intense colors are generally less affected by surroundings than tints, shades, and mixtures. Small areas of color are more subject to perceptual changeability than large areas.

At this point it will be useful for you to secure a package of colored papers. Using simple patterns of three or four colors, play with the idea of changing the appearance of a color by the use of various background colors. With a hole punch you can make many small circles of color very rapidly. Lay pieces of one color against several different background colors, and look for combinations that show the most striking differences. If a few colors show such complicated relationships, think how profoundly complex the painting of a picture becomes! Nearly a century ago John Ruskin aptly warned beginning painters:

> Every hue throughout your work is altered by every touch that you add in other places; so what was warm a minute ago, becomes cold when you have put a hotter color in another place, and what was in harmony when you left it, becomes discordant as you set other colors beside it.[2]

8-2. Simultaneous contrast. The gray circles are all identical in value.

BORDER CONTRAST

In Figure C-4a you will notice that each band of color seems to be lighter on the side of its dark neighbor and darker on the side of its light neighbor. The longer you look, the greater the effect becomes. If you reach a point of real doubt, take two pieces of paper and cover all but one band: you will once again see it as a uniformly colored area. This effect is called *border contrast*, since it occurs at the border between one color and another. The same effect also occurs among different hues (Figure C-4b): the central bands show on each edge the warm glow of its neighbor on the opposite side. As with simultaneous contrast, the net perceptual effect is to maximize apparent contrast, here in border zones.

C-1. Larry Poons. *Northeast Grave.* Acrylic, 90 by 80 inches,
1964. (Permission Hirshhorn Museum and Sculpture Garden,
Smithsonian Institution.)

C-2. Look steadily at the center of the pattern while counting slowly to sixty. Then look at the black dot on the right and wait for the negative afterimage to appear.

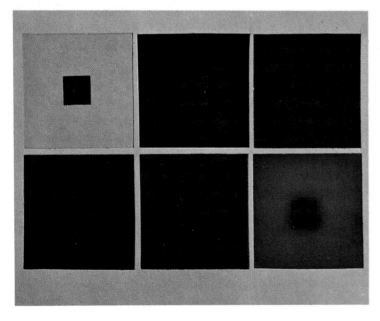

C-3. Simultaneous contrast. The center squares are all identical in color.

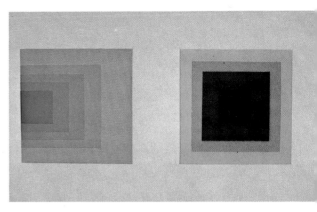

C-4. Border contrast.

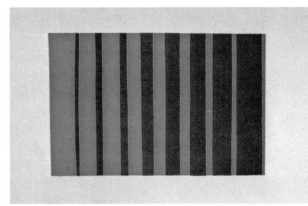

C-5. Vibration.

C-6. Transparency.

C-7. Georges Seurat. *Port-en-Bessin*, Entrance to the Harbor. Oil on canvas, 21⅝ by 25⅝ inches, 1888. (Collection The Museum of Modern Art, New York. Lillie P. Bliss Collection.)

C-8. Willem de Kooning, *Woman I.* Oil on canvas, 75⅞ by 58 inches, 1950–52. (Permission Museum of Modern Art, New York.)

C-9. Richard J. Anuskiewicz. *All Things Do Live in the Three..* Acrylic on composition board, 21⅞ by 35⅞ inches, 1963. (Permission Mr. and Mrs. Robert M. Benjamin, New York.)

CONTOUR CONTRAST

Figure 8-3 appears to show a lighter circle on top of a darker circle. But in fact, both circles have the same value. The only real variation is a very small area of shading along the outer edge of the smaller circle. You can test this illusion by covering the edge of the smaller circle with a string. The string sits on top of a uniformly colored large circle! This effect also occurs in Figure 8-4.

The contour-contrast illusion can be found in Oriental painting and ceramics dating as far back as a thousand years ago. It is especially effective for enhancing the apparent brightness of images such as the moon or snow-covered mountains (see Figures 8-5 and 4-8). This illusion can be effectively rendered with airbrush or watercolor techniques—a simple, soft definition of a contour gives the illusion of brightness or volume.

Why these illusions occur is not fully understood. Simultaneous and successive contrast seem to involve the nature of the cone cells themselves, while border and contour contrast may relate to an interaction of excitatory and inhibitory influences in adjacent cone cells.

8-4. *A Lohan with One Attendant.* Ming Dynasty. (Courtesy Museum of Fine Arts, Boston.)

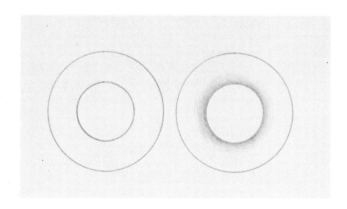

8-3. Contour contrast.

8-5. Sansetsu. *Snowscape* (a six-panel folding screen). 1590–1651. (Permission Museum of Fine Arts, Boston.)

VIBRATION

The shimmering effect in Figure C-5 is called *vibration*, because the edges of the shapes appear to vibrate. This type of optical activity occurs most dramatically when the colors involved are complementary or nearly complementary in hue, intense, and of the same approximate value. The zone of optical activity is along edges or contours, so the vibration effect is enhanced by the presence of many edge zones.

Why vibration occurs is not clear, although it seems to relate to the dynamics of paired complementary colors, to the effects of simultaneous and border contrast, and possibly to the rapid tremors of the eye. Because color vibration is an intense, aggressive effect, it is often exploited in commercial advertising and psychedelic posters. In the hands of a skilled optical artist, the effects can be so intense that you may automatically squint, as if in the presence of a too-bright light!

COLOR IN BLACK AND WHITE

If you spin a cardboard disk with a black-and-white pattern, you will see colors while the disk is in motion! The patterns in Figure 8-6 are effective, although nearly any pattern with relatively equal amounts of black and white will do. Blacks vary in effectiveness (e.g., Magic Marker, ink, paint, black paper), and the effect is apt to be more pronounced under fluorescent light. This phenomenon sometimes appears on a black-and-white television set, and you may see shades of pale pink or blue. Why this effect occurs is not fully understood, but if the Hering theory is correct, these sensations of color could result from the excitation of color receptors adjacent to black-white receptors—which is brought on by the rapid and continuous movement of an image across the retina.

TRANSPARENCY

When three colors occur together and the middle color appears to be a mixture of the other two, it may be read as two transparent colors superimposed on one another (Figure C-6). With judicious color selection this effect can represent degrees of depth: one surface may seem to pass either through, on top of, or below the other. When it is combined with a simultaneous portrayal of overlapping and continuous contours, the perception of transparency is unavoidable. The percept is a further extension of our tendency to see complete and continuous forms wherever possible.

OPTICAL MIXTURE

From a distance we cannot clearly perceive the edges of small shapes (Figure 6-8). Similarly, from a distance small areas of color seem to blend into one another and are seen as a mixture rather than as separate hues. This effect is called *optical mixture*, and it occurs within the eye rather than in the pigments.

This effect was the focus of experimentation for a group of painters called the pointillists, who theorized that optical mixture would provide a more dynamic expression of color than the traditional pigment mixtures. Carrying the concept to an extreme, they carefully constructed their paintings with small dots or points of unmixed colors (Figure C-7). Close-up these canvases look like colored confetti—but at various viewing distances the colors blend and forms emerge. Pointillism was a slow, methodical process, and as a painting technique it generally lacks the liveliness and brilliance we encounter in the more spontaneous brushwork of other impressionists.

Color-printing processes take advantage of optical-mixture effects. When you look closely at a printed color picture, you can often see tiny dots of several different ink colors. In a four-color process the basic inks commonly used are magenta, cyan (a blue), yellow, and black. The combination of dots in these three primaries plus black gives us the illusion of a full range of color and shading!

PSYCHOLOGICAL DIMENSIONS OF COLOR

Color evokes moods, expresses feelings, and even affects our physical sense of well-being. Imagine cooking dinner in a bright red kitchen on a sweltering summer day; going to sleep or waking up in a vivid orange room; sitting in a classroom with black walls. Evidence indicates that our feelings about color may result to some extent from measurable physiological responses. Exposure to red, for instance, has been found to speed up heart and respiration rates and to raise blood pressure. Blue, on the other hand, reduces blood pressure, pulse, and respiration rate. Institutions such as schools, hospitals, and public office buildings have traditionally decorated with toned-down, faded wall colors—an apparent effort to create a neutral environment that will not offend anyone. Studies have found, however, that for people who must spend long periods of time in such environments, these "institutional colors" tend to be not inoffensive but actually depressing. Many schools, hospitals, and nursing homes are now discovering that more lively colors on the walls lift the morale of both patients and workers.

While some colors appear to affect people in general physiological ways, other human responses to color are arbitrary, personal, or socially influenced. Cultural tradition determines the symbolic meanings of colors. In our culture, for example, white represents purity, but for the Chinese it is the color of death. Clergy of the Judeo-Christian tradition wear black, but Buddhist monks wear saffron orange. In some groups married women may wear nothing but neutral colors.

8-6.

COLOR ASSOCIATIONS

Gray is not composed of primary colors but of black and white, the "noncolors." In this sense it reflects a certain uninvolvement or noncommitment. We associate it with cloudy skies, gray days, the "blahs." Grays can be restful for short periods, but over long spans of time the color deprivation may be depressing.

Physiologically, blue is calming, restful, serene, and cool. Environmentally, we associate it with sky, water, space, and distance. In some cultures blue is used to create an environment for meditation.

Red is a strong, warm, committed color, the color of blood and fire, associated with strength, passion, and affirmative action. Red attracts attention and is used for this purpose in traffic signs, red-pencil corrections, and clothing accessories. Because red is such a strong color, it is rarely used in large, unrelieved areas but more often as an accent.

Yellow is bright and cheerful, lighter and less dense than red: the color of sunshine, light, and radiant energy. Unclear or impure mixtures of yellow, however, can seem harsh, unhealthy, or repulsive.

Green universally symbolizes growth, expressing fertility and the yearly renewal of plant life on the earth. It has been called the color of "elastic tension," conveying the qualities of both energy and evenness that are present in its components of yellow and blue.

Violet is often associated with mysticism and fantasy. Environmentally, it is the color of increasing distance and space. Violet, composed of red and blue, is subject to wide variation in hue and can seem either warm or cool, depending on its dominant component.

Brown is the color of earth, but also of dirt and mire. Brown can seem earthy, cosy, and fertile or dirty and dull. Like gray, brown is often considered to be a neutral color, but of warmer sensibility, since it is a mixture of the primary colors.

Black is enigmatic—often seen as expressing negation, annihilation, void, or mystery. But the darkness of black—like the darkness of night—can also be warm, engulfing, sheltering, and comforting.

These associations to color are easily rendered irrelevant by specific situations. Consider your differing reactions to a red apple and a red room, a green lawn and green bread, or a violet evening gown and violet skin! In general, color relates psychologically to the *affective* or emotional dimensions of a perceptual experience. Beyond the simple information or data level, color enriches the subjective, nonrational aspects of our experience.

COLOR AND ART

Artists have always been restricted in their use of color by economic conditions, technical knowledge, and the culturally assigned roles of color at different periods. The first pigments and dyes were made from things people found in their immediate environment: colored earth, minerals, and substances from plants, animals, and burned materials. Where trade developed, artists could secure pigments and dyes from other places.

Until fairly recently, an artist had to prepare his own paint by grinding dry pigments and mixing them with a liquid vehicle—a slow and painstaking procedure that spawned its share of guarded secrets and mysterious formulas. Painting was not something you engaged in on the spur of the moment. To those of us who are used to solving the paint problem by a trip to the local store, the diversity of materials used in the past is astonishing: it includes such things as gum arabic, egg yolk, milk, wax, and a large number of variously treated oils and resins. Oil painting as we know it was not technically possible until after 1400 and did not assume any kind of universality until the seventeenth century.

Some cultures have supported the symbolic use of color, but the western tradition has limited artists to representing object color—a restriction consistent with the commitment to the retinal image as the source of realism. Object color expresses color constancy, and we are responding to that when we say that an artist uses color "realistically."

The impressionists of the 1800s were the first to perceive and use color in a different way. They were excited by newly developed theories and discoveries in optics, the branch of physics that deals with the nature and properties of light and vision. The impressionists knew that light striking the retina is diffracted to form the colors we see, and they believed that black in a painting was artificial, since dark colors and shadows were actually caused by a complex of color interactions. The impressionists sought to paint light as it actually registered on the retina—objectively, with an "innocent eye." In their effort to portray the truth of the visual experience, they painted out-of-doors, and they painted ordinary people—they worked at recording what they actually saw, rather than painting a compsition intellectually constructed in the studio.

Although this approach may not strike you as particularly daring, it was a remarkable departure from the conventions of the time, which were dominated by the French Academy of Fine Arts, a national school that specified the education of artists and sponsored and judged the major exhibitions. The Academy works of that era exhibit such refinement in the modeling and illusionary painting of objects and bodies in space that when they are reproduced they almost look like composed photographs. The Academy preached a strict studio approach: art must be elevated from everyday life; figures must appear in classical or mythical settings; the composition must show careful arrangement by a rational intellect. The revolutionary impressionists rejected all of these conventions. They painted everyday people in everyday settings; their compositions suggest the spontaneity and chance elements of candid snapshots; and their brushstrokes are shockingly visible. In spite of the scientific detachment embraced by the impressionist philosophy, their integrity to the visual experience reflects a joy and vitality that has endeared them to succeeding generations of viewers.

Although the impressionists broke away from the conventions of object color, their approach remained inextricably bound up with the retinal image. Certain painters found this and the role of detached observer too confining for their own sensibilities. Gauguin and van Gogh, in particular, felt that color by itself—apart from its atmospheric origins—could express something. For these artists using color to express personally felt emotion involved a greater integrity than using color derived from objective observation. These and other artists, including Matisse, who used color in emotional and "unrealistic" ways, were hysterically termed the fauves—wild and dangerous beasts.

The fauves liberated color from the retinal image and thrust it into the arena of emotion. Even with its distortions of form, however, fauvism remained committed to *representational* painting—the portrayal of identifiable things existing in the objective world. Going a step further, the abstract expressionists rejected the necessity of objective representation, and began to use paint and color to express emotion with a purity and abstraction uncontaminated by objective imagery (Figure C-8). The major abstract expressionist painters, including Jackson Pollock and Willem de Kooning, were well-schooled in traditional, realistic drawing techniques. Their work does not reflect lack of ability in the conventions of art but rather a deep and profound disenchantment with the expressive possibilities inherent in the representational approach.

Most recently, the optical artists have disengaged color from even these basic emotional qualities in order to manipulate the pure perceptual properties of color, unrelated to feeling, emotional expression, or symbolic value. They have given us an art depending for its effect solely upon the universal physiology of the human eye and brain—essentially a "culture-free" art. Eskimo, Frenchman, Aborigine, Russian, Japanese, African, American—all can see and respond to optical paintings with the same perceptual processes, for these works do not depend on the cultural education of vision but only on your willingness to look and to respond (Figure C-9).

In the history of color, each point of liberation eventually became a fixed commitment that was found too confining by another group of artists. The growth of art is like that of the chambered nautilus, which ever outgrows its shell and continually pushes outward, building a new and larger space in which to grow.

9. THE IMPLICATIONS:

Getting It Together

THE MYTH OF INSTANT REPLAY

Sometimes people think of visual perception as operating something like a television camera recording a scene on a tape that is labeled and filed in the brain. If someone asks what you did last Friday night, you go to your mental file, retrieve the tape dated "last Friday," and the process of memory unfolds as a replay in your mind. Our legal system lends support to this concept in the courtroom when a person's fate is determined by the "replay" capability of an eyewitness. However, several recent studies show that eyewitness memory—in both real and simulated situations—is shockingly vulnerable to manipulation by personal, emotional, and social stresses: the very words in which a question is asked or the order in which a lineup is aranged can determine the way a memory will be reconstructed!

The concept of the mind as an objective recorder is based on a false premise about the purpose of perception. The study of visual perception clearly reveals that perceptual processes are not structured to record data but rather to organize meaning. Sense data are not perceived as isolated fragments: the mind organizes them in meaningful and relevant ways. In memory storage sense experiences are assimilated into a total accumulation of meaning and association. An event is reconstructed, or remembered, from its interwoven relationships with other memories.

In comparison to the "instant-replay" notion, this operation might at first seem to be a weakness. But for the most part it functions as an advantage—if you had to record and maintain all data as separate fragments, you would soon become immobilized under the burden of dealing with a continual bombardment of inputs. Perceptual programming for meaning prevents you from expending time and energy on separate stimulations as if they were unique and unrelated to other experience. Perception is a streamlined survival process. The miracle of the mind is that it copes so well with a jumble of inputs and is able to organize percepts so that—most of the time—your world is reasonably coherent, predictable, and stable. By regarding perception as a program for *processing*—not for recording—data, you can understand why there is often great disparity among the meanings we assign to experience.

DATA REDUCTION

Perception is selective: it does not admit all data willy-nilly into your head. Metaphorically, perception functions rather like a net whose mesh size allows only certain things to pass through. In this way the sense organs act as "reducing valves" that simplify or screen out certain aspects of the objective world. Some psychologists refer to this as a process of *data reduction*.

Data reduction occurs at the first point of visual contact with the objective world: the retina. The retina screens out almost all of the electromagnetic radiation that surrounds you: it responds only to wavelengths between four hundred and seven hundred billionths of a meter. Similarly, your ears screen out all frequencies except those between twenty and twenty thousand cycles per second. In each instance you are able to directly encounter *only* the active energy within a limited range. Imagine the alternative: what chaos there would be inside your head if at this very moment you were consciously receiving inputs from all the radiation around you—UHF, VHF (all channels), AM, FM, shortwave (all frequencies), X ray, infrared, ultraviolet, and heaven knows what—all at once! Most of us have a problem simply making sense out of hearing two radio stations at the same time! Fortunately, visible light limits us to a specific energy range—the range we assume to be the most significant for our survival. Technology has already invented machines that respond to some other energy wavelengths. ESP research and new experiments with such things as Kirlian photography may eventually reveal aspects of the energy spectrum that are now barely imaginable.

When a minute portion of visible light contacts the retina, it activates or stimulates the retinal cells, which in turn activate cells in the brain. Recent research suggests that brain cells, too, are limited to specialized—not generalized—responses: it appears that sensory stimulation is transformed in the brain into codes involving combinations of specific cell responses. On a simple level, the problem is rather like having forty speech sounds and only twenty-six alphabet letters. All the sounds cannot be encoded unless some letters function as the code for more than one sound. The correct sound then has to be inferred from context, serial order, and/or past learning. Since the number of cells in a single brain exceeds the total population of the earth, the possibilities of the brain's coding circuitry appear endless, even if an "alphabet" is phylogenetically determined. This represents a very different concept from that of the brain as a copy machine, since it means that events and experiences are not stored in the brain by a duplicating process but rather are encoded into a data bank. Along with this it is important to recognize that brain cells never contact an objective stimulus: they are in touch only with cell inputs from the eyes and other organs and with fellow brain cells.

Further efficiency accrues because the brain processes stimulations at a level that does not usually involve your conscious awareness. Before you can even become aware of an objective stimulus, it must be reduced to visible light by your eye and processed by your brain into a perception. This means that you are not in direct contact with your sensory stimulations—they enter your consciousness only as manifest perceptions.

Even though the contact you have with an objective stimulus is subjected to extensive data reduction and processing, your perceptions generally prove reliable, because they are formulated by the brain on the basis of statistical probabilities. Perception, then, is a series of automatic, tentative judgments about probable meaning and relevance as extrapolated from limited data. Thus, a percept is an inference from a range of possibilities—not from a fixed point of certainty. Perception, like physics, operates on the uncertainty principle, and final judgments must evolve from more complex intellectual processes. Seeing is not ipso facto a reason for believing!

A LITTLE HELP FROM YOUR FRIENDS

Not only are your perceptions organized phylogenetically in the eye-brain-mind circuit, but they are further organized by the culture in which you live. A common foundation of perception and experience among members of a group is essential for its survival—only then can there be a basis for communication and cooperation. Speech is the most obvious basis for a shared language among any group of people: words structure experience and establish a starting point for shared consciousness. The parable of the Tower of Babel articulates this: the destruction of a group's single language so confused people that they could no longer continue building their tower. To experience the extent of your own cultural conditioning, try to look at the following *without* seeing words or letters:

Maple Road Next Right

On the other hand you will find it easy to see this 美 as a pattern of brushstrokes, although a Chinese will read "beautiful" as easily and as inevitably as you read "Maple Road."

The need for shared perception is fundamental to the human condition. Sharing experience reinforces your own perception and lends credibility to your own experience. How often do you say (or hear) phrases such as, "I know what you mean," "I had the same feeling," or "Dig it"—expressions of mutual reinforcement. In fact, when a person's perceptions are so far out of the ordinary that others cannot easily share them, that individual is considered "way out in left field," "hung up," or legally "insane." Whenever an individual's perceptions are significantly different from those of other people, the credibility of the group is challenged: either the individual's views must be rejected or the group views must be reexamined. Unhappily, history shows that the former often proves more expedient than the latter.

While it is easy to see that written and spoken languages are culturally learned, it is not so easy to comprehend that other aspects of perception are culturally trained as well. Differences in sense perception have not been as extensively researched as differences in language, but the studies that have been done reveal significant findings. For example, it has been found that not all cultures read depth in pictures that use vanishing-point perspective or differential size (Chapter 6). Music that does not conform to our familiar chromatic scale is at first perceived as dissonance or noise—not as harmony. These observations, as well as studies of cultural perception of space, suggest that the social conditioning of perception is far more extensive and complex than is generally thought.

THE ARTIST AND THE ESTABLISHMENT

For a good portion of human history few people have been able to do what you are doing at this very moment and taking very much for granted: reading a written language. Historically, it was the artist who reflected important percepts of the culture by means of public images. The artist was valued for his ability to encode cultural perceptions into an integrated visual language. For example, ancient Egyptian art cherishes detail and predictibility in the activities of human beings (Figure 4-16). Oriental art manifests philosophical dualities as a harmony of positive and negative elements (Figures 3-12, 3-15, and 4-8). The ancient Greeks perceived the human body as a matrix for balance, harmony, and rationality (Figure 9-1). Western art since the Romans (except for the Middle Ages) articulates specific points in a space-time continuum. Only recently has the written word usurped the power of the visual image as a direct influence on the majority of people.

9-1. *Venus de Milo.* Greek, early 1st century B.C. Plaster cast from the original marble in the Louvre Museum, Paris. (Collection The Slater Memorial Museum, Norwich, Connecticut. Photograph by the author.)

Consequently, the immortality of an artist depended on a happy convergence of his perceptions with the perceptions of the culture in which he lived and worked. Throughout most of history the artist depended on patrons in the heart of the establishment—usually the ruling class or the church—to support him and to commission his work. Leonardo de Vinci might well have been dismissed as an irrelevant eccentric in an ancient Chinese civilization. Marc Chagall (Figure 5-7) or Willem de Kooning (Figure C-8) would not have been valued by the Romans, who focused on specific historical events and accurate portraiture. Because of this we have no way of knowing how many unknown individuals throughout history created images that expressed no significant meaning either for their contemporaries or for the historians who followed. To be meaningful, visual language, like verbal language, must establish a point of shared experience.

Many factors have contributed to the decline of the artist as a handmaiden in the service of cultural perpetuity and have changed the role from that of spokesperson to that of challenger. The industrial revolution, bringing mass-produced goods, has made hand craftsmanship less essential and less valued. Photography has simplified the making of an image into an instantaneous process. The prevalance of literacy has provided alternate channels of communication and influence. As a result the artist has moved from the central core of our culture into the frontier areas.

THE PROBLEM FOR THE ARTIST

In the past a person's sex and the economic and social conditions into which the person was born programmed options to a greater extent than is true today. To become an artist, a person would need to show promise and to have an influential connection to secure an apprenticeship in the studio of an established artist. Over a period of years he would undergo rigorous and rigidly specified training in technique and materials. The opportunity to work on his own would depend on finding and convincing a patron to underwrite and finance his work. Only if he were very lucky indeed might he be commissioned to individually conceive and super-

vise the execution of his own masterwork. The lives of many old masters show evidence of deep stuggles to reconcile their integrity with the opinions of a patron who held the purse strings.

Since the impressionists rebelled against the French Academy, things have been very different. The decision to be an artist is now a highly individual one, often made in the face of counterpressures from others. It is a commitment that values integrity to oneself more than an economic and social security that would involve compromise. Culturally, the creative artist now appears to be an independent renegade, a self-appointed and sometimes quixotic challenger of the establishment. Why, then, does a person become an artist?

We might begin to answer this question by looking at the problem of an individual's need for meaning in relation to the cultural structures of meaning. Some theories of creativity suggest that artists perceive aspects of a stimulus that are outside its generally accepted meaning and that they perceive conflicts of meaning among stimuli. Less creative persons simply tune out or ignore these dissonant perceptions, but a creative person is driven to resolve them, to unify them—to restructure the percept or concept until it makes sense. This urge to synthesize disparate elements is characteristic of creative innovators in all fields: science, philosophy, literature, history, psychology, social reform—as well as the arts.

Before the artist (or scientist) can pinpoint inadequacies in the existing structure, he or she must have rigorously explored those traditions, must have become frustrated by them, must know exactly where the dissonance exists. At that point the artist is like any other thinker who finds no existing statement capable of expressing the new perception of order, so a new theory or rationale is invented.

For the major innovators in art the established visual forms become an inadequate language for dealing with certain kinds of perceptions, so they invent new forms. Until the abstract expressionists, for example, no western art form could express a pure emotion disembodied from specific objects— a concept made all the more tenable by the growth of psychological theories that posited free-floating emotion. Since all art forms (except decorative design) were based on the representation of objects, a new form had to be invented. The frequent public criticism of "modern artists"—that they can't draw—is based, for the most part, on ignorance. An examination of the lives of the major abstract expressionists reveals that they received vigorous training in traditional skills and media and that it was their very familiarity with the "tools of the trade" that exposed the limitations.

Today's artists face somewhat the same problem with respect to time and change. Traditional art forms are static, unmoving: they do not use change and time as structural elements, even though they may make statements *about* them. Some contemporary artists are now inventing forms in which the very activities of change and time are as integral to the work as paint or canvas. The need for the artist to articulate this concept and for the public to assimilate it is especially meaningful now when we have to deal with the "future shock" of accelerating change within our lifetime.

When the artist acts as a challenger or a pioneer in relation to the values of the culture, he or she develops problems with the public. Communication must start from a point of shared experience, and the public is often more concerned with covering up the dissonances and weaknesses in the status quo than in recognizing them. When an artist works on what he or she sees as a fundamental problem in a frontier area, people frequently have difficulty recognizing a point of shared concern: the artist seems to be working in a "world of his own." An example of this is de Kooning's obsession with image creation through a process of destruction (Figure C-8). Other painters, however, found this a meaningful philosophical problem and a phenomenon frequently experienced during the painting process. For some years de Kooning was considered a "painter's painter."

The same situation also occurs in other fields. A scientific researcher may spend a lifetime working on a seemingly obscure question: collecting data, conducting experiments, searching for an answer. To the scientist such explorations have profound implications for larger, basic questions in the field, and while these may not be recognized by the public at large, they can be appreciated by other scientists. Barnett Newman's involvement in placing a single stripe on a canvas is such a case in art (Figure 9-10). For Newman, the division of pictorial space at the simplest, most fundamental moment of confrontation had consequences for image making. How irrelevant this concern seemed to a nonartist is revealed in the following anecdote.

Franz Kline and Elaine de Kooning [two well-known contemporary artists] were sitting at the Cedar Tavern when a collector Franz knew came up to them in a state of fury. He had just come from Newman's first one-man show. "How simple can an artist be and get away with it?" he sputtered. "There was nothing, absolutely nothing there!"

"Nothing?" asked Franz, beaming. "How many canvases were in the show?"

"Oh, maybe ten or twelve—but all exactly the same—just one stripe down the center, that's all!"

"All the same size?" Franz asked.

"Well, no; there were different sizes; you know, from about three to seven feet."

"Oh, three to seven feet, I see; and all the same color?" Franz went on.

"No, different colors, you know; red and yellow and green ... but each picture painted one flat color—you know, like a house painter would do it—and then this stripe down the center."

"All the stripes the same color?"

"No."

"Were they the same width?"

The man began to think a little. "Let's see. No. I guess not. Some were maybe an inch wide and some maybe four inches, and some in between."

"And all upright pictures?"

"Oh, no; there were some horizontals."

"With vertical stripes?"

"Uh, no, I think there were some horizontal stripes, maybe."

"And were the stripes darker or lighter than the background?"

"Well, I guess they were darker, but there was one white stripe, or maybe more..."

"Was the stripe painted on top of the background color or was the background color painted around the stripe?"

The man began to get a bit uneasy. "I'm not sure," he said, "I think it might have been done either way, or both ways maybe..."

"Well, I don't know," said Franz. "It all sounds damned complicated to me."[1]

THE PROBLEM FOR THE VIEWER
FINDING COMMON GROUND

Before an artwork can "speak" to you, you must find some meaningful aspect that you can relate to. On the surface art from the past gives you fewer problems, for, if nothing else, you have some concept of its historical context: it is sandwiched between the works that came before it and the ones that followed. You know how things turned out— how the issues were resolved. A work seen from a distance in time can be appreciated for its place in the order of things. This, however, is an intellectual approach.

Perception, rather than intellect, is the raw material through which the artist and the viewer communicate. Perception is the code or language in which an artist transmits an idea as well as the process by which the viewer receives and decodes it. Just as different spoken languages are constructed from grammatical arrangements of sounds, so different visual languages are made up of visual elements in syntactical relationships. You would think it absurd to hear someone call all books written in French "garbage," simply because that person could not read the language. And yet it is not unusual for people to dismiss whole categories of art simply because they do not reflect a familiar visual language!

One of the difficulties in trying to approach artworks with an "innocent eye" is that cultural programming and personal experience give you a perceptual *expectancy*, or *set*, which means that whenever possible you will see what you expect to see. Perceptual programming for meaning tends to create self-fulfilling prophecies out of visual encounters. Once you realize that many culturally determined perceptions are simply preprogrammed and arbitrary organizations of sense data, you are ready to try to go beyond that expectancy by temporarily suspending judgment. This means tuning

in to what is actually happening with your perceptual processes and keeping your busybody mind from giving you ready-made and premature closures.

Ask yourself these kinds of questions when you look at an artwork. What is the significance of the artist's choice of image or subject: is it intimidating, irritating, scary, complex, formal, serene—or what? Does the object's "personal space" draw you closer, perhaps invite you to touch it—or do you sense that a specific distance is called for? Trust your feelings; you can usually assume that your reactions—if they are free from prejudice—are the ones the artist intended you to have.

Look for the perceptual processes that the artist has chosen to activate. Is the image sharp and specific, or does it have ambiguities; if so, where? Is the image "normal" (reflecting form constancy), or does it embody distortions? Does the work manipulate size or color constancy; in what way? How does the artist organize the figure/ground relationship? The field/frame relationship? How is space and distance shown (or denied)? What depth cues are used and—equally important—what cues are *not* used? How is color used: perceptually; according to constancy; atmospherically; symbolically; opulently or sparingly? Answers to questions like these help you decode the values manifest in the art object. If an image is unsharp and lacks detail, the artist is expressing ambiguities or generalities rather than a specific or unique situation. When brushstrokes are "invisible," paint becomes an illusion of something other than itself; when they are visible, the artist has included something of the active process of creation as a part of the meaning structure. This is true for sculpture too: highly polished surfaces conceal process; tool marks or structural visibility reveal process. When you involve yourself with these dimensions, you allow the work to engage you perceptually; you let it talk to you.

Figures 9-2 and 9-3 show two historical works of art to which you can relate these kinds of questions. Figure 9-2 is a sculpture of the Roman emperor Augustus, done about 20 B.C. The image shows us a man who is healthy and well-proportioned, embodying a kind of heroic normalcy. He is nearly seven feet tall—somewhat larger than life—and elevated on a pedestal so that you must physically look up to him. The perception of his size is further enhanced by a size-constancy relationship with the cherub and the dolphin, whose small size by contrast increases Augustus' apparent largeness. Cover up the cherub with your finger and you will see how effectively this device works. The sharp, concrete details in clothing reveal that Augustus was studied by the artist at close range—not from afar. The face is somewhat idealized, yet it is an accurate likeness of a specific person. Augustus is in the process of taking a step forward—

a pregnant moment suggesting mobility in space. He reaches out, gesturing to a point outside his personal-space "bubble" as if hailing someone—perhaps a viewer. All these perceptual aspects are consistent with the Roman concept of a ruler: an approachable man (not a god, although governing under divine mandate), moving about in real space with superior power and heroic strength, a military conqueror (his clothing) with a certain humility (his bare feet), greeting those whom he rules with a certain formal friendliness.

The Pharaoh (Figure 9-3) exhibits a different rendition of a ruler. The smooth surface of the

9-2. *Augustus of Primaporta*. Marble, Roman, 80 inches high, c. 20 B.C. (Permission Vatican Museum, Rome.)

9-3. *Colossal Alabaster Statue of Mycerinus*. Egyptian, 2599–2571 B.C. (Permission Museum of Fine Arts, Boston.)

stone and the lack of surface detail reflect the perception of someone seen from a distance. Getting close to this sculpture does not reveal more visual detail—a perceptually defined distance remains no matter how close you come. Although this is a portrait, physical imperfections and irregularities are not revealed; it is difficult even to determine his age, for he is not marked by a process of growing older. The pharaoh is in a balanced, symmetrical posture, an alert repose, engaged in no particular emotion. He looks as if he might have been sitting there for quite some time and perhaps will continue to do so for quite a while longer. He appears so contained in his personal-space "bubble" that you can come close to this sculpture—even touch it—and yet feel that you have not penetrated his personal space. Through the language of perception this work manifests a man-god, set apart from other people, untouched by time, existing in an impenetrable space. Such works continue to be important and satisfying because the perceptual experience acts as a pipeline to the consciousness of another culture.

In another type of encounter, anthropologist Edward T. Hall delightfully describes how the active perceptual exploration of an artwork led him to a new dimension of understanding.

For many years I had never really appreciated Rembrandt's knowledge of vision. Increased understanding came unexpectedly one Sunday afternoon in the following way. Visually, Rembrandt's paintings are very interesting and tend to catch the viewer in a number of paradoxes [Figure 9-4]. Details that look sharp and crisp dissolve when the viewer gets too close. It was this effect that I was studying (how close could I get before the detail broke down) when I made an important discovery. . . . Experimenting with the viewing of one of his self-portraits, my eye was suddenly caught by the central point of interest in the self-portrait, Rembrandt's eye. The rendition of the eye in relation to the rest of the face was such that the whole head was perceived as three-dimensional and became alive *if viewed at the proper distance.* I perceived in a flash that Rembrandt had distinguished between foveal, macular, and peripheral vision! He had painted a

stationary *visual field* instead of the conventional visual world depicted by his contemporaries. . . . The eye must be permitted to center and *rest* on the spot that he painted most clearly and in greatest detail at a distance at which the foveal area of the retina (the area of clearest vision) and the area of greatest detail in the painting match. When this is done, the registry of the visual fields of both the artist and the viewer coincide. It is at this precise moment that Rembrandt's subjects spring to life with a realism that is startling. . . .[2]

9-4. Rembrandt van Rijn. *St. John the Evangelist.* Oil on canvas, 40¼ by 33 inches, 1606–69. (Permission Museum of Fine Arts, Boston.)

ACCEPTING THE CHALLENGE
Hardest of all for many people is the art of the present day. It is safer to suspend judgment when reacting to works of the past: you learn about yourself in relation to people of past times. But when you interact with contemporary works, you learn about yourself in relation to your present-time world. To

make matters more difficult, art tends to reveal weaknesses in cultural structure: it will run through a cultural loophole as water spurts through a crack in a dam. Comments like "That's not art," "I don't know why they show such junk," and "Artists can't paint anymore" usually reflect a preference for plastering up holes rather than dealing with structural weaknesses.

Art of the present is conceived and born of the present. It makes little sense to apply outdated standards to it. We don't expect a modern playwright to compose Shakespearean prose, and we don't look to our scientists to operate with cosmic notions of an earth-centered or even a Newtonian universe. Why do people put art in a separate category? One reason is that our schools do not educate us to expect changing visual language as they do changes in scientific theory. Another is that science engages us on an intellectual level, a step removed from our personal lives. Art, however, involves the raw data of living—the validity of our perceptions, both private and cultural. That's a lot more threatening.

Just how basic such an experience can be was revealed to me by an encounter with the work shown in Figure 9-5. The sculpture stood in the lobby of a museum, and as I passed through I remember vaguely noticing a large woman standing there loaded with shopping bundles. Her appearance was oddly different from that of the usual museumgoer, but I dismissed the prejudice and hurried on by. Later, when I returned to the lobby, I saw the same woman standing just as I had left her. Incredulously, I realized that this was not a woman but a shockingly lifelike scupture. Approaching it, I felt uncomfortable, as if I were invading the personal space of a real person. As I forced myself to study the details of her physiognomy at very close range, I became even more ill at ease, as if I were staring with fascination at the flaws and curiosities of a real stranger's body. I felt furtive and ready to look away instantly so as not to be caught in the act. It would have been easy to dismiss these feelings, yet by lingering and exploring the discomfort I experienced a profound complex of personal and cultural inhibitions about personal space. It was a minisession in sensitivity training.

When an art object can have a powerful impact on a viewer's consciousess in this way, the question "But is it art?" seems somehow trivial. When the power is there, the art is there.

When you look at contemporary art, focus on two dimensions: (1) what are the issues that concerned this artist, and (2) what do your perceptions tell you as you try to experience them in an unprejudiced way? Try to view an artwork in relation to the intent

9-5. Duane Hanson. *Young Shopper.* Polychromed polyester resin and fiberglass, with clothes and other apparel, life-size, 1973. (Property, Dr. Edmund Pillsbury, New Haven. Photograph by Eric Pollitzer, courtesy O. K. Harris Gallery, New York.)

will help you develop visual imagination. Such imaging may suggest quite original ideas for art or craft projects.

FRAGMENTS

How much visual information is necessary before you can recognize what you are looking at? You can explore this question by sectioning off very small parts of a photograph with finders (wide L-shaped pieces of white paper used to frame a small area). By expanding, reducing, and changing the shape of the framed area, you will discover which fragments reveal the identity of the whole image and which seem meaningless.

An interesting drawing, painting, or photograph can be developed by enlarging a fragment at one of these critical points. In general, compositions tending toward the minimum essentials engage a viewer more actively, since supporting information from the viewer's own mind must be added to make closure. With too much visual information (redundancy), the composition is less likely to hold a viewer's attention.

FOUND WORDS: FOUND MEANING

Randomly selected words have a startling power to suggest profound and unusual ideas. Try listing every tenth word from a passage in a book or magazine until you have about twenty-five words. Cut the list apart and rearrange the words until you arrive at a meaningful sequence using all the words in the list.

If you don't give up (this exercise takes patience!), you will experience the astonishing degree to which words and their associations are fluid and unfixed and the extent to which syntax and sequence determine meaning. This activity contributes to creative thought in much the same way as the Projections exercise above.

GETTING INVOLVED WITH THE EYE
EYE CONTEXT

The image of a human eye elicits a profound response. Experiment with this dramatic impact by creating images using eyes in abnormal or unexpected ways. It is easy and fun to make collages from magazine photographs: cut out eyes and put them on other pictures—upside down on a face or in a plate of spaghetti; put human eyes on animals; eliminate eyes completely or erase parts of them. Or carefully paint or découpage a rock or an egg to simulate an eyeball and put it in some surprising context. Eyes also make a startling and unusual motif for a stitchery patch or articles such as pincushions (ouch!), jeans, or glasses cases. (For examples of artists' use of eyes, see Figures 2-1, 2-2, and 2-3.)

EYE ASSOCIATIONS

Keep a running list of all the phrases and terms you encounter that use eyes or vision as a way of expressing nonvisual ideas. You will discover the extent to which vision seems necessary to express other dimensions of human experience. (For starters see Chapter 2.)

AFTERIMAGE

Divide a blank piece of paper in half. On one half place a simple, bold design; leave the other half blank except for a dot in the center (see Figures 2-7 and C-2). By experimenting with different patterns and colors you can experience reciprocal color relationships originating in the retina. Afterimage effects can also be planned and integrated into paintings (Figures 2-8 and C-1).

SHIMMER

Simple tools such as felt-tip pens and french curves can be used to create active, shimmering patterns—effects favored by some optical artists (Figures 2-14 and 3-17). Your work needs to be neat and accurate for effective results.

EYES IN ART

Artists use eyes to express meaning, to focus dramatic impact, or to direct the path of the viewer's gaze within the composition. You will find it enlightening to make a point of noticing eyes in a number of different artworks: cover up the eyes or imagine them looking in a different direction (see Figures 2-3, 4-4, 5-7, 5-14, 6-5, 6-6, 6-13, 6-16, 7-7, 7-8, and C-8).

EYE CONTACT

Eye contact as a method of silent communication is an interesting study in human behavior. For example, how do people react when you refuse to establish eye contact while talking to them? How do teachers make use of eye contact in the classroom? How do people communicate with eye contact as they pass each other on a busy sidewalk or in a busy hallway?

A carefully kept journal of eye-contact observations will give you some insights into nonverbal modes of human communication.

DOTS

The mosaic pattern of cell stimulation in the retina has been compared to an image constructed of dots, such as a newspaper photograph (Figure 2-6). The size of the dot unit determines the amount of detail that can be resolved in the image.

Try to make a drawing using only dots that are all equal in size and blackness (no lines!). Represent shadows and depth by dense dot areas; show lighted and raised areas by spreading dots further apart. By not relying on familiar line and shading techniques, you will become more sensitive to the way you perceive images. Drawing from life rather than imagination will develop your power of observation.

GETTING INVOLVED WITH THE BRAIN
FIGURE/GROUND

Alternating figure/ground relationships can be used in designing for any medium—collage, painting, photography, textiles, drawing, crafts (see Figures 3-7, 3-8, 3-9, and 3-10). Using the negative (or ground) spaces in letters as positive (or figure) space is a good way to handle designs with words or letters, such as monograms, trademarks, posters, or holiday cards. You can also make the ground visually active—an approach often found in the work of Vincent van Gogh and Edvard Munch, as well as in some psychedelic posters.

The figure/ground relation helps you to organize an integrated and unified design by making you account for each space in a lock-and-key pattern.

PERIODIC PATTERNS

Optical artists in particular have often structured dramatic compositions from identical or similar units repeated in a regular and predictable pattern. By themselves many periodic patterns cause optical effects (Figures 2-13, 2-14, 3-17, 3-18, and 3-19). By superimposing two or more periodic patterns a new pattern may be perceived (Figure 3-19). When two patterns are superimposed, a moiré pattern will emerge from intersections in which angles are less than 30 degrees (Figures 3-19 and 3-20).

You can organize periodic patterns in many media, for example, ink, colored papers, paint, textile designs, collages, or reliefs using industrial die sheets. Printmaking offers a natural medium for repeating identical units. Superimposed periodic patterns can be constructed in both two- and three-dimensional relationships. You will find templates, Zip-a-Tone, and other technical drawing materials especially useful.

GROUPING

To make closure, your mind groups small units that are close together and relatively meaningless in themselves. The effect occurs in high-contrast photography (Figures 3-13 and 3-14), Zen brush painting (Figure 3-15), and situations in which the image is interrupted (Figure 3-12). You can experiment with grouping by constructing an image from abstract units such as dots or lines; by arranging segments of a cut-up picture; by translating a photograph into a drawn or painted image consisting only of black and white areas.

Because the separation of the units requires "filling in the blanks," your experiments with constructing a meaningful image from component parts will help you to experience visual organization as a determining factor in perception.

BINOCULAR VISION

Binocular vision is the basis for several novel and dramatic demonstrations. Experiment with giving each eye a different image simultaneously. If possible, your brain will fuse both into a single image: a birdcage and a bird is this type of pair. By placing an ordinary index card vertically between the two images and viewing them at close range, you can often cause fusion to occur. Much more effective, however, is a stereopticon (Figure 5-4), in which you can fit images into the cardholder.

When images or colors are too unrelated to one another, the viewer experiences an image that continually and spontaneously rearranges itself (retinal rivalry). An effective way of producing retinal rivalry is to make a pair of cardboard spectacles, using one lens of red cellophane and the other of green cellophane. In this case retinal rivalry will be caused by different color inputs. When you look through the spectacles at a simple red-and-green geometric pattern (e.g., green squares on a red background), the pattern will dance, alternating between black and white. With the spectacles you can look around and discover other situations of retinal rivalry.

GETTING INVOLVED WITH CONSTANCY
TRACE
This exercise is a way to see the world in the perspective of da Vinci (Chapter 6) and Dürer (Figure 6-16). Find a piece of window glass, Lucite, acetate, or some other transparent material and a felt pen or grease pencil that will mark on it. Tape the transparent material onto a window or secure it vertically so that it is held firmly in place. Hold your head still and look with one eye through the glass at the scene beyond. Pretend you are actually seeing a two-dimensional image projected onto the glass and outline the objects with the marker. You will be recording the image the way the retina and the camera record it.

This exercise helps you to identify the profound compensation imposed on the retinal image by size constancy. If you are learning traditional, realistic drawing techniques, this activity helps you learn to discount size-constancy effects.

CONTEXT
Size constancy relies on surrounding context for cross-referencing size/distance relationships. When these relationships are unusual or unexpected, you feel confused: the experience is sometimes termed *surreal*. Unreal size relationships are often used in advertising (e.g., the giant fingers that "do the walking through the Yellow Pages"), as well as by surrealistic artists such as Magritte (Figure 4-6).

You can use magazine photographs to make surrealistic collages that violate normal size relationships with dramatic or shocking results. First, look for a photograph to act as a background: this will set the scene. Then cut out objects from other photographs to place within the scene. By slitting the background picture in selected places you can create the illusion of real depth by overlapping (e.g., with slits along hilltops you can put things behind the hills; with a slit in the mouth you can insert things in it).

Another way to explore the effect of context is to make a series of photographs of a common object that normally comes in a range of sizes (a pumpkin, a doll, an iron skillet, for example). Make the object appear larger or smaller by putting it in different environments and/or by using different camera viewpoints.

By manipulating size relationships you increase your sensitivity to context clues.

BLOWUP: POP
Some pop artists do not include in their compositions the normal surroundings of a familiar object: the object appears enlarged far beyond its normal size because nothing within the picture field normalizes it.

Try making a drawing or painting of something in which the field/frame relationship excludes the normal visual context. (I once saw a delightful blowup of a small section of a Juicy Fruit gum package.) Working with field/frame relationships sensitizes you to scale and context as factors in the illusion of size and distance.

FORM NORM
Choose an object and draw it carefully from observation from at least four different viewpoints (or photograph it from several positions). Overlay each drawing or photograph with tracing paper and outline *only the silhouette* of the object in each one. Now study the silhouettes. Which presents the most identifiable view? This reflects the mental norm of form constancy. Which is the most difficult view to identify?

This exercise will alert you to the importance of

viewpoint selection in portraying objects. A view approximating a mental norm prompts easy closure; a view deviating markedly from the norm makes closure more difficult (Figure 4-14).

MIND'S EYE
Observe and draw a subject (such as a still life or a patient person) from one viewpoint. Contour-line drawing is a good technique because it requires careful observation and accuracy. Remain in the same position and make a second drawing based on how you *imagine* the subject would look from a position on the opposite side of the room. Then go to the imagined viewpoint and compare your drawing to the subject as it actually looks.

This technique brings your form constancies into play by directing your mind to the hidden parts of objects. Convincing drawings always reflect the artist's awareness of the unseen as well as the seen (Figure 5-14).

GETTING INVOLVED WITH SPACE
PEOPLE IN SPACE
Keep a daily journal for a week or two in which you describe observations of people in relation to their personal space. Look for unspoken signals that tell you when you are too close to someone. Describe strategies that individuals use to increase or decrease distance from one another. Observe seating arrangements in different situations and analyze how they function to define the distance between people. Watch people protecting their personal space in public places such as elevators, buses, and subways.

Listen for comments about the space in your own home—the needs, complaints, and fantasies of the people you live with. Such comments as "You can't turn around in here" and "I dream about a house with lots of light and space" reveal how well or badly a space meets the needs of the individuals who inhabit it. These observations will help you plan ideas for redesigning or rearranging some of the living spaces in your home.

A way to find out how people visualize space is to ask several people to draw you a map giving directions for how to get to some specific location. As any lost traveler knows, people differ markedly in self-confidence, clarity, and organization and in the degree to which they use detail and visual symbols.

All these activities help sensitize you to how people behave in relation to the "hidden dimension."

MOTION PARALLAX
Motion parallax as experienced by a moving viewer is an important element in some contemporary artworks (Figure 7-12). You can experiment with motion parallax on a small scale by separating two or more transparent, patterned surfaces by a small distance. Use such things as layers of glass or transparent plastic, petri dishes, clear-lidded plastic boxes, or Lucite photocubes. You can also construct a relief surface of accordion-folded posterboard or wood strips glued to a backing. Draw or paint patterns or images on more than one surface or plane. As you change position, the relationships between the patterns also change.

SUBJECTIVE PERSPECTIVE
This exercise is a special way of drawing that starts with the self. Using a large piece of drawing paper and a strong, dark contour line, begin at the lower edge of the paper by drawing what is next to the top edge of the paper. Then draw what appears next to that, and continue drawing each thing in turn, working systematically outward from yourself. The drawing will develop and unfold in its own way, showing a distinctive vitality unlike that of conventional perspective. This slow and careful process forces you to carefully observe the visual relationships of objects in the space immediately surrounding you.

GETTING INVOLVED WITH DEPTH AND DISTANCE
TRACE
If you want to clarify your understanding of vanishing-point vision, cut from magazines or newspapers several photographs that appear to have vanishing points. Make a tracing of each photo, projecting the dominant lines until they converge on the horizon line. This convergence will often occur outside the borders of the picture. The tracing will reflect the vanishing-point relationships as a function of the camera's location in space.

ABSTRACT LANDSCAPE

Make an abstract collage from torn and/or cut colored paper or tissue paper. Ty to incorporate *all* the following methods of showing space and distance: overlapping, position on the picture plane, size gradient, and color gradient. Give the *feeling* of a landscape without showing any recognizable objects. In this way you will compose space and distance effects using the laws of visual perception without relying on representational imagery.

GRADIENT

Abstract gradient systems can create a powerful illusion of three dimensions (Figures 4-13 and C-1). Make your own experiments with this kind of depth illusion using pens, markers, templates, paint, paper, fibers, or other media.

CHIAROSCURO

Chiaroscuro was a favorite technique of Renaissance artists (Figures 5-14 and 6-13). Try drawing from observation, using no lines—only patterns of light and dark to show form and volume. A good subject would be a still-life arrangement of common objects such as tin cans without labels, egg cartons, cardboard boxes, draped fabric, etc. Avoid patterned or textured objects: plain surfaces show gradients best. Use a lithographic crayon, a regular crayon with the paper removed, charcoal, or india ink—these can render sensitive gradations of light and dark over broad areas easily. Avoid linear drawing tools. This approach will help you study patterns of shadow and illumination and develop your ability to produce illusions of volume and form without depending on line.

ANALYSIS

Look at paintings by a number of different artists. Carefully analyze all the methods of showing space and depth used in each work. This exercise helps you evaluate for yourself the role played by vanishing-point relationships in the portrayal of depth and distance.

GETTING INVOLVED WITH MOTION

SPINNING DISK

Any pattern viewed in motion exhibits qualities that are different and often unexpected compared to its motionless state. Colors blur, combine, and sometimes seem to glow or flash. Certain patterns, such as eccentric rings, appear to move independently of the motion of the pattern plane. Radial patterns may show a wagon-wheel effect—seem to rotate in the opposite direction. You can make your own experiments in pattern movement by cutting from lightweight cardboard several disks five or six inches in diameter. Decorate them with different kinds of patterns made with Magic Marker or colored paper. Spin them on a straight pin stuck into a pencil eraser or on a bent paper clip. Small electric motors rheostatically controlled, lazy susans, and phonograph turntables are other ways of putting the pattern into motion. The artist Marcel Duchamp was fascinated by this problem and evolved many patterns with startling and unexpected effects (see Bibliography).

MAKING TRACKS

Tracks are marks left by something moving across a surface. Some tracks communicate a strong sense of the motion that made them. Chinese brush painting and calligraphy expose the speed, direction, and pressure of the brush (Figure 3-15). The abstract expressionists also used this effect (Figure C-8). You can experiment with this quality of motion by using india ink and a bamboo brush. Another technique is to apply printing ink to a string, place it between two pieces of paper, and pull it out under a certain amount of pressure. The movements of the string will be recorded with much the same effect as a multiple-exposure photograph of a moving subject. Such experiments often create energetic images that are visually exciting.

NATURAL FORCES

Consider the possibilities of an artwork using some natural force as a source of motion. Mobiles, windmills, weather vanes, whirligigs, and wind chimes use air currents (Figures 7-6 and 7-13). Some things will float languidly in liquids of high viscosity (such as the old-fashioned snowstorm paperweights).

Iron filings change patterns in response to magnets. Magnets attract and repel one another as if they were alive. Static electricity causes particles to cling, especially to plastic. Heat from the sun makes a radiometer spin, and heat from a candle moves the delicate Swedish Christmas chimes. The momentum of a swinging weight causes chickens to peck on a wooden paddle. Try making your own project.

FLIP

The flip book creates an illusion of motion by a fast succession of images, each only slightly different from the preceding one. Even a simple shape such as a circle becoming gradually smaller or more elliptical makes a surprisingly effective illusion. Be sure to test the "flipability" of the paper. Index cards work well; so does lightweight oak tag and certain drawing papers. You will need twenty-five to fifty pages for a good effect. When you make a flip book, you must analyze and divide up the stages of the motion into a series of minute changes.

FILM

An animated film can be made in several ways. The conventional technique is to shoot only a few frames of a still subject, make slight changes, and shoot a few more frames, etc. This kind of animation can be done with drawings, collage pieces, clay, or bendable toys and is easily accomplished with a super-8 home-movie camera. Drawing or scratching directly on the film acetate is another technique used imaginatively by the Canadian film artist Norman McClaren. This requires 16 mm clear leader with Magic Marker—super-8 frames are too small for this method unless you have the vision of a watchmaker and the patience of a saint.

Remember that approximately twenty-four frames are used in *one second* of viewing time. The most common beginner's fault is too rapid motion. Making an animated film requires a well-organized plan; a number of helpful books for beginning filmmakers are on the market.

GETTING INVOLVED WITH COLOR
PERCEPTUAL COLOR

You can explore simple color effects such as afterimage (Figure C-2), simultaneous contrast (Figure C-3), and vibration (Figure C-5) with ordinary construction paper. But if you are more serious about experimenting with color, you should buy a package of papers made especially for this purpose (Color-Aid is one brand). These papers are about six by nine inches in size, and a package contains approximately 200 *different* colors! The papers are expensive, but as they provide you with a nearly infinite number of choices and combinations, you will be able to do a phenomenal amount of experimenting and will develop very fine color discrimination. Exercises with this type of paper should be small in scale so that you never completely use up a sheet of color—for that would eliminate it from your range of choices. Some paper manufacturers also make acrylic paints that can be mixed to match the papers, and some artists use the papers to plan larger paintings. A good sourcebook for perceptual-color exercises is Josef Albers' The *Interaction of Color* (see Bibliography).

OPTICAL MIXTURE

One way to explore optical mixture is to do the Dots exercise above with colored fine-tip felt pens, which will give you an effect similar to that of pointillist paintings (Figure C-7). You can also work with strokes, as most of the impressionists did. Use pastels or Cray-pas on dark-colored construction paper; do not use any rubbing, smearing, or blending techniques, and do not use any black strokes. You will learn much more if you work from observation—not from a drawing or photograph. Working from life forces you to make your own color decisions. When you copy, the decisions have already been made, and you learn to match color—not to perceive it.

COPY OF A MASTER

You can learn a good deal about mixing and matching paint colors without having to cope with all the other problems of making a painting by copying a painting reproduced in a book. Make a tracing of the main areas in the painting and with carbon paper transfer the tracing to a piece of unstretched canvas or mat board. Choose the pigments you think you will need from a paint manufacturer's chart, preferably with the aid of a teacher. In almost all cases *only* four to five colors plus black and white are necessary: the color unity and harmony in the work of professional artists is often due to a carefully chosen but surprisingly limited palette.

Place a piece of window glass over the picture in the book and on the glass mix your paints to match the colors in the book. When you have matched a color, apply it to the canvas.

Needless to say, it is the better part of wisdom to choose a work where the color areas are rather well defined. Although this may seem mechanical, it is an excellent way of getting well acquainted with specific pigments and their mixtures, as well as becoming familiar with the details and nuances of a particular work of art.

SCHEME

Color schemes can be organized in several ways for fashion, interior design, weaving, quilts, or stitchery projects. Traditional color-wheel combinations can be used, but more exciting and unusual schemes can be planned around perceptual effects (e.g., transparency, vibration, contour contrast, etc.). Another way to organize color schemes is by theme (e.g., summer, autumn, the beach, outer space, Times Square). A color scheme based on a single well-defined season or environment has a built-in integration and harmony.

DYE

In our modern age, we usually use color without any awareness of the pigment's origin. Surprisingly good dyes can be made from ready sources such as onion skins. Happily, information on making natural dyes is now easily available from inexpensive, informative publications. When you make your own dyes, you also acquire some botanical knowledge about your environment. And one of the great pleasures of dye making is simply being outdoors, finding and gathering plants.

Tie-dye, batik, and painting with dye are popular home projects. These techniques are generations old, and with a little research you can quickly become involved with the art and design of different cultures.

BIBLIOGRAPHY

BASIC READINGS IN ART AND PERCEPTION

Arnheim, Rudolph. *Art and Visual Perception: A Psychology of the Creative Eye*. Berkeley: University of California Press, 1954.* Significant contribution to the psychology of art; a clear, direct explanation of how the eye organizes visual material.

Arnheim, Rudolph. *Visual Thinking*. Berkeley: University of California Press, 1969.* Develops the hypothesis that visual perception is a cognitive activity and that the traditional distinction between sense and thought is false and misleading.

Barrett, Cyril. *An Introduction to Optical Art*. New York: Studio Vista, E. P. Dutton and Company, 1971.* A comprehensive series of plates.

Boring, E. G., Langfeld, H. S., and Weld, H. P. *Foundations of Psychology*. New York: John Wiley and Sons, 1948. This basic text is especially interesting and clear in its presentation of principles and research in the field of sense perception.

Chipp, Herschel B. *Theories of Modern Art: A Source Book by Artists and Critics*. Berkeley: University of California Press, 1968.* A collection of fundamental documents of twentieth-century art, selected for their value in explaining basic theories and concepts beginning with postimpressionism.

Fontein, Jan, and Hickman, Money L. *Zen Brush Painting and Calligraphy*. Boston: Museum of Fine Arts, 1970.* An enlightening and inspiring text and series of plates for readers seriously interested in the history and spirit of Zen brush painting.

Gibson, James J. *The Perception of the Visual World*. Boston: Houghton Mifflin Company, 1950. Standard work by a pioneer in the study and definition of visual gradients.

Gombrich, E. H. *Art and Illusion: A Study in the Psychology of Pictorial Representation*. Princeton: Princeton University Press, 1969.* One of the major contributions to the relation between art and perception; very readable and profusely illustrated.

Gregory, R. L. *Eye and Brain: The Psychology of Seeing*. New York: McGraw-Hill Book Company, 1966.* Fascinating, comprehensive discussion of visual perception, based on research in physiology and psychology.

Gregory, R. L. *The Intelligent Eye*. New York: McGraw-Hill Book Company, 1970.* Develops the hypothesis that perception is modified by symbolic patterning; emphasizes three-dimensional perception and includes a good deal of material on stereoscopy and 3-D drawing.

Mayer, Ralph. *The Artist's Handbook of Materials and Techniques*, 3rd edition. New York: Viking Press, 1970. Standard reference; encyclopedic coverage of materials and methods, primarily for painting.

Mueller, Conrad G., Rudolph, Mae, and the Editors of Life. *Light and Vision*. New York: Time, Inc., 1966. Light and lively coverage; lots of pictures and an interesting, readable text.

Newhall, Beaumont. *The History of Photography*. New York: Museum of Modern Art, 1964.* Fascinating chronology of the development and impact of photography, with attention to technicalities of the medium; profusely illustrated.

Parola, René. *Optical Art*. New York: Van Nostrand Reinhold Company, 1969. Visually dramatic demonstrations of optical-art effects, profusely illustrated with work by both professional artists and high-school students.

Russell, John. *The Meaning of Modern Art*. New York: Museum of Modern Art, 1974. A vividly and beautifully written series explaining the individual, social, and philosophical issues that determined the direction of art since the impressionists; lavishly illustrated.

Sze, Mai-Mai. *The way of Chinese Painting*. New York: Vintage Books, Random House, 1959.* The philosophy and traditions of Chinese painting, with extensive illustrations of techniques reproduced from *The Mustard Seed Garden*, a seventeenth-century painting manual.

Wilson, John Rowan, and the Editors of Time-Life Books. *The Mind*. New York: Time-Life Books, 1964. Readable, interesting coverage of the neurology and psychology of the mind, accompanied by picture essays.

Woodworth, Robert S., and Schlosberg, Harold. *Experimental Psychology*, revised edition. New York: Holt, Rinehart and Winston, 1954. Complete, concise, comprehensive review and authoritative interpretation of research and theory in perception as well as other fields of experimental psychology; standard text and invaluable reference.

Vernon, M. D. *The Psychology of Perception*. Baltimore: Penguin Books, 1962.* Comprehensive, nontechnical explanation of perceptual processes.

PERCEPTUAL DEVELOPMENT

Beadle, Muriel. *A Child's Mind: How Children Learn from Birth to Age 5*. Garden City, New York: Doubleday and Company, 1970. A readable survey of research in the behavioral sciences, clearly described and integrated for the lay reader.

Bower, T. G. R. *Development in Infancy*. San Francisco: W. H. Freeman and Company, 1974.* Astute analysis of perceptual and cognitive development in infants by one of the noted researchers in the field.

Piaget, Jean. *The Child's Conception of the World*. Totowa, New Jersey: Littlefield, Adams, and Company, 1969.* An exploration of the stages of thought children go through in trying to make sense out of the world, by one of the most significant contemporary psychologists.

Piaget, Jean. *The Construction of Reality in the Child*. New York: Ballantine Books, 1954.* Detailed observation and analysis of the infant's developing perception of objects, people, space, and time.
(See also Robert L. Fantz, Empirical Studies.)

EMPIRICAL STUDIES

Barron, Frank. "The Psychology of Imagination," *Scientific American*, September 1958.[1] Discussion of studies on creativity and originality, the relation of creativity to psychological health, and the characteristics of creative individuals.

Björk, Lars E. "An Experiment in Work Satisfaction," *Scientific American*, March 1975. A social psychologist describes a Swedish experiment organizing work teams in a manufacturing plant as a solution to the repetition and boredom of assembly-line mass production.

Buckhout, Robert. "Eyewitness Testimony," *Scientific American*, December 1974. The reliability of eyewitness testimony is shown to be shockingly low in both simulated and real-life situations. Contributing factors are discussed and analyzed in an interesting and lucid way.

Chapman, Loren J. and Jean. "Test Results are What You Think They Are," *Psychology Today*, November 1971. A discussion and study of the problem of clinicians' own projections onto projective-test results.

Deregowski, Jan B. "Pictorial Perception and Culture," *Scientific American*, November 1972. Tribal African subjects' responses to various representations of depth, together with art styles of other cultures, suggest that depth is not universally perceived in perspective drawings but is a function of cultural conditioning.

Fantz, Robert L. "The Origin of Form Perception," *Scientific American*, May 1961.[1,2] A study of form perception and visual acuity in human infants, birds, and other animals.

Festinger, Leon. "Cognitive Dissonance," *Scientific American*, October 1962.[1] Discussion and study of how people try to meaningfully resolve psychologically inconsistent information.

Gibson, Eleanor J., and Walk, Richard D. "The 'Visual Cliff,'" *Scientific American*, April 1960.[2] Now-classic study of visual depth perception in infants of several species.

Harmon, Leon D. "The Recognition of Faces," *Scientific American*, November 1973. Study on the amount of information required for the recognition of individual faces. The visual material is very interesting; the text is concerned primarily with technical details and computer factors.

Heron, Woodburn. "The Pathology of Boredom," *Scientific American*, January 1957.[1] A study of the effects of sensory deprivation and isolation of human volunteers.

Ittelson, W. H., and Kilpatrick, F. P. "Experiments in Perception," *Scientific American*, August 1951.[1] A review of the now-classic experiments in visual perception by Adelbert Ames, Jr., including the distorted room and the rotating trapezoidal window.

Loftus, Elizabeth. "Reconstructing Memory: The Incredible Eyewitness," *Psychology Today*, December 1974. Because of the tendency of memories to integrate, the reconstruction of a memory at a later date is shown to be devastatingly influenced by subtle suggestions in leading questions.

Witkin, Herman A. "The Perception of the Upright," *Scientific American*, February 1959.[1] The now-classic tilting-room experiments in body orientation; defines field-dependent and field-independent perceptual styles and relates them to personality, age, and sex.
(See also Hans Wallach, Motion; and Edwin Land, Floyd Ratliff, and W. A. H. Rushton, Color.)

OPTICS

Asimov, Isaac. "I Can't Believe I Saw the Whole Thing!" *Saturday Review*, September 2, 1972. An explanation of holograms.

Edmund Scientific Company, 300 Edscorp Building, Barrington, New York 08007: *Catalog* No. 752. Free catalog full of marvelous things, including materials for demonstrating visual phenomena. Holograms are available at a cost of approximately six dollars.

Gluck, Irvin D. *Optics*. New York: Holt, Rinehart and Winston, 1969. Chapter 6, "The Eye," explains the physiology and optics of the eye, including a discussion of common vision defects and their correction.

Lasers and Light: Readings from Scientific American. San Francisco: W. H. Freeman and Company, 1970.*

McCarthy, Denis. L. *Holographic Course* (Laser Tech No. 30). Elmira, New York: Laser Tech, subsidiary of Systomation, 1972.* A short text designed for a lecture-laboratory course at the high-school and college level, covering the fundamentals of the laser, general holographic theory and development, and details for conducting holographic experiments. Although this book claims to present material on an elementary level, I recommend it only for readers with a basic foundation in physics and mathematics.

Rainwater, Clarence. *Light and Color*. New York: Golden Press, 1971.* Simple, accurate, illustrated explanations of scientific concepts involving physical and perceptual aspects of light and color. An unusually good guide for the layman.
(See also Edwin Land, Color.)

THE BRAIN
Asimov, Isaac. *The Human Brain: Its Capacities and Functions*. Boston: Houghton Mifflin Company, 1963. Fascinating and thorough explanation of the structure and function of the brain, written with clarity and broad relevance, a characteristic of this popular writer.

Pribram, Karl H. "The Brain," *Psychology Today*, September 1971. Rather technical discussion of a holographic hypothesis of brain functioning, particularly in regard to perception and memory. (Adapted from Pribram's book *Languages of the Brain*. Englewood Cliffs, New Jersey: Prentice Hall, 1972.)

SPACE
Chermayeff, Serge, and Alexander, Christopher. *Community and Privacy: Toward a New Architecture of Humanism*. Garden City, New York: Doubleday and Company, 1963. Problems and solutions in urban planning in relation to human and ecological values, written in a style and format that is clear, visual, and imaginative.

Hall, Edward T. *The Hidden Dimension*. Garden City, New York: Doubleday and Company, 1966. An anthropologist describes the multisensory perception of space, differing sensory worlds among different cultures, patterns of private and public space in various countries, and the implications of perceptual and psychological space for urban planning; very readable.

Mulvey, Frank. *Graphic Perception of Space*. New York: Van Nostrand Reinhold Company, 1969. A programmed-learning format visually demonstrates the principles of producing illusions of depth and distance.

Nishihara, Kiyoyuki. *Japanese Houses: Patterns for Living*. San Francisco: Japan Publications, 1967. Fascinating examination of Japanese houses as an expression of societal and human needs, materials, and methods; includes parallels and contrasts with Western residential forms. Gorgeous photographs, sensitive text.
(See also Eleanor J. Gibson and Richard Walk, Empirical Studies.)

MOTION
Brett, Guy. *Kinetic Art: The Language of Movement*. New York: Reinhold Books, 1968.* A brief, humanistic discussion of the history and issues of time, space, motion, and viewer involvement in art, with emphasis on the work of individual kinetic artists.

Cook, Olive. *Movement in Two Dimenions: A Study of the Animated and Projected Pictures which Preceded the Invention of Cinematography*. London: Hutchinson of London, 1963. Fascinating, detailed survey of the visual illusions and inventions that entertained masses in the past.

Muybridge, Eadweard (Lewis S. Brown, ed.). *Animals in Motion*. New York: Dover Publications, 1957. Over four thousand individual photographs illustrating phases of motion in horses, dogs, cats, lions, kangaroos, deer, and twenty-eight other animals.

Muybridge, Eadweard. *The Human Figure in Motion*. New York: Dover Publications, 1955. Over four thousand seven hundred individual photographs, chosen for their value to artists, doctors, and researchers.

Myers, John Bernard. "Puppets: Dance and Drama of the Orient," *Craft Horizons*, December 1974. An illustrated article briefly describing the legends, stories, and cultural significance of oriental shadow and rod puppets.

Wallach, Hans. "Perception of Motion," *Scientific American*, July 1959.[1] A discussion of the visual perception of motion, emphasizing the importance of relationships within the visual field.

COLOR
Albers, Josef. *The Interaction of Color*. New Haven: Yale University Press, 1971.* Text of the original edition with a few selected plates. A way of studying and teaching color using perceptual experience rather than mechanical systems, by a leading twentieth-century colorist.

Land, Edwin. "Experiments in Color Vision." *Scientific American*,

September, 1958. A pioneer researcher in the mechanism of color perception describes and analyzes some of his experiments.

Luscher, Max (Ian A. Scott, trans.). *The Luscher Color Test*. New York: Random House, 1969.* Popular color-preference test based on the theory that a person's color choices reveal psychological dynamics; includes general discussion of color psychology and its applications.

Ratliff, Floyd. "Contour and Contrast," *Scientific American*, June 1972. A discussion of neural mechanisms possibly responsible for subjective contour and contrast perceptions that are inconsistent with objective luminance. Photographs and diagrams from both art and science make this article especially interesting.

Rushton, W. A. H. "Visual Pigments and Color Blindness," *Scientific American*, March 1975. A technical explanation of some experimental evidence on the nature of anomalous color vision. (See also Clarence Rainwater, Optics; and Peter Farb, Miscellaneous.)

ARTISTS

Hess, Thomas B. *Barnett Newman*. New York: Museum of Modern Art, 1971.* Biography and works of a major formalist painter.

Hess, Thomas B. *Willem de Kooning*. New York: Museum of Modern Art, 1968.* Comprehensive, illuminating biography of a major abstract-expressionist painter.

Instituto Geografico de Agostini. *Leonardo da Vinci*. New York: Reynal and Company, 1956. Tremendous number of illustrations interspersed with brief, well-organized text.

Koningsberger, Hans, and the Editors of Time-Life Books. *The World of Vermeer: 1632-1675*. New York: Time-Life Books, 1967. Life and times of the "Sphinx of Delft" and his contemporaries of the Dutch Golden Age, including notes on the nature of realism in painting and the infamous Vermeer forgeries.

O'Connor, Francis V. *Jackson Pollock*. New York: Museum of Modern Art, 1967.* An exhibition catalog with a detailed chronology of the artist's life, drawing freely on Pollock's own statements as well as those of critics and friends.

Soby, James Thrall. *René Magritte*. New York: Museum of Modern Art, 1965.* Catalog of work by the well-known twentieth-century surrealist, who frequently violated principles of size constancy to generate dramatic imagery.

Tomkins, Calvin, and the Editors of Time-Life Books. *The World of Marcel Duchamp: 1887-1968*. New York: Time-Life Books, 1966. Life and times of a great genius of the modern era.

Wallace, Robert, and the Editors of Time-Life Books. *The World of Van Gogh*. New York: Time-Life Books, 1969. Life and times of one of the most popular postimpressionist painters.

MISCELLANEOUS

Farb, Peter. "People are Talking," *Horizon*, Winter 1974. Entertaining reading on theories of the genesis of human language, with a particularly interesting section on patterns of color terminology in various languages.

Luce, Gay Gaer. *Body Time: Physiological Rhythms and Social Stress*. New York: Bantam Books, 1971.* Time structures and daily rhythms that may be important for health and comfort; nontechnical and comprehensive.

Luce, Gay Gaer, and Segal, Julius. "Current Research on Sleep and Dreams," Public Health Service Publication No. 1389. Available at a cost of less than a dollar from the Superintendent of Documents, U.S. Government Printing Office, Washington, D.C.

Luce, Gay Gaer, and Segal, Julius. *Sleep*. New York: Lancer Books, 1966.* Nontechnical, entertaining, comprehensive discussion of sleep research.

Packard, Vance. *The Hidden Persuaders*. New York: Pocket Books, 1958.* Now-classic expose of how advertisers exploit psychological and perceptual research to manipulate the public.

Perls, Frederick, Hefferline, Ralph F., and Goodman, Paul. *Gestalt Therapy: Excitement and Growth in the Human Personality*. New York: Dell Publishing Company, 1951.* Compelling presentation of the Gestalt method and theory of personality, accompanied by reader-participation experiments.

Toffler, Alvin, and McHale, John. "The Future and the Functions of Art: A Conversation," *Art News*, February 1973. Interesting, extemporaneous conversational fantasies about art forms of the future.

Wells, H. G. *The Country of the Blind*. A short story about the adventures of a lost traveler who finds himself in a village where the inhabitants have been blind for generations; his sight proves to be a handicap.

*indicates an inexpensive paperback edition.
[1]Reprinted in *Frontiers of Psychological Research: Readings from Scientific American*. San Francisco: W. H. Freeman and Company, 1966.
[2]Reprinted in *The Nature and Nurture of Behavior: Developmental Psychobiology: Readings from Scientific American*. W. H. Freeman and Company, 1973.*

Note: Most articles published in *Scientific American* are available as separate offprints. For a complete listing write W. H. Freeman and Company, 660 Market Street, San Francisco, California 94104.

FOOTNOTES

CHAPTER 1
1. Bach, George R., and Wyden, Peter. *The Intimate Enemy: How to Fight Fair in Love and Marriage.* New York: Avon Books, 1968.

CHAPTER 2
1. Gombrich, 1969, page 113 (see Bibliography, Basic Readings).

CHAPTER 3
1. Gregory, 1966, page 49 (see Bibliography, Basic Readings).
2. Toffler and McHale (see Bibliography, Miscellaneous).

CHAPTER 4
1. Soby, 1965 (see Bibliography, Artists).

CHAPTER 5
1. Piaget, 1954, page 2 (see Bibliography, Perceptual Development).

CHAPTER 6
1. Instituto Geografico de Agostini (See Bibliography, Artists).
2. Gombrich, 1969, page 222 (see Bibliography, Basic Readings).
3. Instituto Geografico de Agostini, *op. cit.*, page 436 (italics mine).
4. *Ibid.*, page 435.
5. Tompkins *et al.*, page 43 (see Bibliography, Artists).

CHAPTER 7
1. Piaget, 1969, page 200 (see Bibliography, Perceptual Development).
2. Adapted from *Webster's New World Dictionary of the American Language*, second College Edition. New York: The World Publishing Company, 1968.
3. Arnheim, 1954, page 371 (see Bibliography, Basic Readings).
4. *Ibid.*, page 366.
5. October 19, 1878.
6. Newhall, page 83 (see Bibliography, Basic Readings).
7. *Ibid.*, page 86.
8. Muybridge, 1957, page 16 (see Bibliography, Motion).

CHAPTER 8
1. Albers, page 23 (see Bibliography, Color).
2. Quoted in Arnheim, *op. cit.*, page 354.

CHAPTER 9
1. Quoted in Wallace, page 33 (see Bibliography, Artists).
2. Quoted in George P. Elliott. *Dorothea Lange.* New York: Museum of Modern Art, 1966, page 6.
3. Quoted in Hess, 1971 (see Bibliography, Artists).
4. Quoted in Hess, 1971, page 89 (see Bibliography, Artists).
5. Quoted in Hall (see Bibliography, Space).

INDEX